MIXED MARRIAGE
and the
JEWISH FUTURE

MIXED MARRIAGE
AND THE
JEWISH FUTURE

by DAVID KIRSHENBAUM

Rabbi, B'nai Moses Ben Yehuda Congregation
London, Ontario, Canada

NEW YORK
BLOCH PUBLISHING COMPANY
The Jewish Book Concern
5718 - 1958

PRINTED IN THE UNITED STATES OF AMERICA
BY VAIL-BALLOU PRESS, INC., BINGHAMTON, N.Y.

The crown of grandparents is their grandchildren

(Ethics)

Dedicated to my beloved grandchildren:

JOEL IRVING GOLDSTEIN

AND

WENDY BELLA KIRSHENBAUM

ACKNOWLEDGEMENTS

I am grateful to the Publication Committee of the Canadian Jewish Congress for its good opinion of this book, resulting in a generous subsidy.

I am indebted to my Congregation B'nai Moses Ben Judah, whom I have served over thirty years, to the Sisterhood and the Tephillin Club, for their material assistance.

Many thanks to the Rabbi Kirshenbaum Book Committee, and especially to my dear friends, A. B. Siskind, Q.C., president, and A. B. Gillick, secretary, for their devoted assistance.

To my wife, Pearl, for her patience and understanding.

FOREWORD

For more than three decades in my capacity as rabbi I have been involved in the problems of the Jewish community. In this time I have gotten to know, with some degree of intimacy, the Jewish home, the Jewish family, and our Jewish youth.

Most of the problems I have encountered in Jewish family life, particularly in provincial centers, have led to the conclusion that there is one major threat to the Jewish family and home, threatening them with complete and utter disintegration. This is mixed marriage.

For years, like many others who realize the full importance of that menace, I carried my thoughts in my heart.

I saw the problem becoming more and more acute, with fatal consequences for the future of our people. Mixed marriages were becoming daily occurrences. Jewish families who felt confident the epidemic could not touch them were thunderstruck when they found the situation in their own group. It would be rare nowadays to find a Jewish family completely free from intermarriage. The disease has been making deeper and deeper inroads; it affects the most reputable Jewish families; it undermines the best rooted and established Jewish groupings.

This book is not a scientific or sociological study, but a cry from one whose house is on fire and who calls desperately for help.

Its purpose is to dispel the apathy of the Jewish public, in the hope that it may save the Jewish home from the destructive fire of mixed marriage.

Why is it that today any problem of the remotest connection with Jewish life receives copious public attention?

There are lengthy essays and articles; conferences are convened; no expense is spared; entire apparatuses of offices and staff are organized. The one problem of mixed marriage, however—a greater threat to Jewish survival than any of the others—is overlooked.

Is it because we are ashamed to mention this disease aloud, or because the sickness has already penetrated so deeply into the Jewish home and family?

Where are our spokesmen, our Jewish national and religious leaders? Where are our rabbis, both traditional and modern? Why are they afraid to preach boldly from their pulpits and raise their voices at rabbinical conferences about the plague that imperils the House of Israel?

The rabbis are certainly interested in Jewish survival. That is their vocation. Mixed marriage will ultimately lead to a situation where their synagogues are empty or transformed into Christian congregations "of Jewish descent."

Do our leaders not realize that unless a strong dam is set up to stop the flood, all other efforts to fortify Jewish life can have no permanence or security?

Have the Jewish community workers who devote themselves to fund-raising and philanthropy ever given thought to how thin the thread that links many Jews with Jewishness —the perfunctory contribution made once a year to the local Jewish Welfare Fund or United Jewish Appeal? Has it occurred to them that with the rise in mixed marriages, even this thread will be severed?

I have frequently participated in arrangements for national Jewish conferences. These assemblies concern themselves with the whole range of Jewish problems. Anything, no matter how trivial, that has a connection with Jewish continuity and survival is given consideration; it is dealt with at length in a paper or treated by an outstanding specialist, followed with a full-dress discussion by the delegates. In all these years I do not remember a single occasion when the problem of mixed marriage was on the agenda in any of these national or religious Jewish assemblies.

The problems of anti-defamation and public relations, to name one instance, very frequently involve lengthy addresses and well-intentioned resolutions. Are they more vital for the future than the problem of mixed marriages?

More than once at planning meetings for conferences, I have raised the question of the plague, and demanded it be placed on the agenda. Many conceded that the problem was serious, but was "too delicate" to be handled publicly. Others impatiently shrugged off the whole matter. "It's not too bad —no cause for alarm, Israel will survive. . . . There have always been mixed marriages among us. The Jewish people have existed and always will exist."

We have touched on this problem with rabbinical colleagues, asking if there were mixed marriages in their communities. Their faces would darken a bit at the query. They would reply in a mixture of apathy and worry, "What can we do? It's an ailment of the land we live in. For obvious reasons we can't deal with the subject from our pulpits . . ."

In these chapters I deal with this vexing and tragic problem, its probable causes, and the unhappy consequences for Jewish parents with whom I have sorrowed. There are broken lives of mixed couples and their children who grow up to be self-haters and Jew-haters, and who despise their parents for the marriage and its consequences. The writer has seen families who have pioneered in the founding of Jewish communities uprooted from their origins and completely submerged in the surrounding non-Jewish world . . .

If this book will impel Jewish parents, Jewish boys and girls, rabbis, national, religious, and communal leaders, and the Jewish public at large, to give some thought to the problem and to the great danger it poses for Jewry and Judaism, and if only one youth, one maiden, one Jewish family be saved—"and their names will not be erased from Israel"— this will be my reward!

CONTENTS

MIXED MARRIAGE
and the
JEWISH FUTURE

CHAPTER I

DECLINE OF THE JEWISH FAMILY

In the days of creation, when the Almighty made the world, the Torah describes not only the emergence of man, but his deeds and conduct. Adam and Eve had children, and the families grew. The Torah lists the children and grandchildren of each generation, telling whence each family was derived, and who their parents and ancestors were. The family tree of Father Abraham is given greater attention and detail in the Torah:

> "When it came to Abraham, it amplified the account, for his family was worthier before God."

The holiness, purity, morality, and decorum of Abraham's family life are contrasted with the life of the nations around him. Abraham's personality as future patriarch of the Jewish people is brought out through his settled family life, the modesty of Sarah, the obedience of his only son Isaac who was ready to sacrifice himself in order to follow his father's command, and the confidence the Divine Will reposed in him for this reason.

> ". . . Abraham shall surely become a great and mighty nation, and all the nations of the earth shall be blessed in him . . . to the end that he may command his children and his household after him, that they may keep the way of the Lord, to do righteousness and justice . . ." (Gen. 18:19).

The difference in behavior of Abraham the Hebrew in that ancient idolatrous time was expressed not only in his

1

monotheistic religion, but even more in the moral phase of his family life. Even Eliezer, his slave, was different from other slaves. He became part of Abraham's family. The master devoted himself to the spiritual and moral side of the family, and Eliezer was the economic administrator. The patriarch of the Jewish people, with his vision to the end of all generations, saw that survival of the Hebrew family was dependent on whether his son Isaac marry a daughter from the "house of his father and land of his birth." So great was his confidence in Eliezer that he assigned this mission to him and abjured him by an oath "not to take a woman from the daughters of the Canaanites." The high morality in family life that Abraham established induced Eliezer to go to Aram Naharaim, ancestral land of his master, and bring thither a bride for Isaac.

Although Eliezer, our sages say, had a daughter of his own and very much wanted to marry her to Isaac, and though as an agent he had a full right to do so, he was convinced that his daughter would not fit in with this family. She would forever remain an outsider; the children would have mixed blood, mixed habits, mixed lives, split personalities. For this reason he carried out the oath he gave his master and thanked the God of Abraham "who had led me in the right way to take my master's brother's daughter for his son" (Gen. 24:48), who should be able to continue the pure, moral family life of Abraham and Sarah. After Isaac brought Rebecca into the tent of his mother Sarah and saw that her modest conduct was the same as his mother's, he was satisfied with the woman Eliezer had chosen for him, ". . . and she became his wife; and he loved her. And Isaac was comforted for his mother" (Gen. 24:67).

Jacob's family life, says the Torah, was full of obstacles, dangers, and struggles. It was difficult for our forefathers to conduct their family life as they wished it, in a world in contrast to this concept. Our ancestors comprehended family life with parents as the foundation of Jewish survival, and the assurance of Jewish continuity.

Before the revelation on Mount Sinai, the most important event in the history of mankind, declares the Torah, was bringing together the family of Moses. Jethro, Moses' father-in-law, brought Moses his wife and children in the desert. The history of the Jewish people is the history of Jewish family life. The Torah, Prophets, Talmud, and Midrash depict the history and the life of the Jewish people in terms of the family.

"At that time, saith the Lord, will I be the God of all the families of Israel. And they shall be my people" (Jer. 31:1).

Our sages comment, "It does not say 'of all Israel' but 'of all the families of Israel,'" from which they conclude that it is family life and moral conduct that make Israel a distinctive people. In our religious works of today we find inscribed not only the greatness and holiness of our kings and heroes, but also considerable detail about their family life; its good and evil, virtues and faults. The prophets and sages saw in advance and understood what sociologists, psychologists, and educators understand and say today, that the family is the very basis of society, the source of the good and the bad in human life.

In biblical times, people were envious of our family life. When Balaam came to curse the children of Israel, he opened his eyes and saw how they dwelt amid their tribes —the beauty and morality of Jewish family life. The doors of the Jewish tents were closed. In every Jewish home there prevailed unity, love, respect, purity. In ecstasy, instead of cursing the Israelites he cried out, "How goodly are thy tents, O Jacob, and thy tabernacles, O Israel!" Pride of family heritage, the glorious chain which stretches from Abraham until today, is one of the main foundations of Jewish folk life. There is a saying in the Talmud, "When God caused His Divine Glory to rest, He caused it to rest only upon families of noble birth." By this our sages meant to express the contrasts of human character, the conduct of the good person and the evil, Isaac and Ishmael, Jacob and Esau. The opinion of our sages, confirmed by the social scientists of our day, is that the character and behavior of a person are dependent on his family, his parents, the kind of training he receives in his home, his early environment. All this is absorbed in a person, along with the foods he digests. It forms the individual and makes him a person. It is an accepted axiom that children in their character and conduct are similar to parents: "The apple does not fall far from the tree." There are, of course, exceptions. Sometimes good families will produce corrupt and degenerate heirs. As the Tenach and the Talmud mention, it was quite possible for Abraham to produce a *para-adam*,* for Isaac to produce Esau, for Eli the priest a Phineas and Hofni, for David an Absalom.

Pride of lineage is not exclusively Jewish. All nations have families who pride themselves on their ancestors; every nation has its aristocrats.

One does not, however, have to be a chauvinist or an exponent of the chosen people theory to admit that there is a great difference between Jewish family pride and that of the other nations of the world. In the case of the latter it is for the most part inflated military and knightly pride arising from the slaughter of people, the enslavement of nations, conquest, war, and devastation. But the Jewish people finds its ideals in our forefathers Abraham, Isaac, and Jacob, the patriarchs of the world. They were the embodiment of goodness, justice, honesty, and gentleness. Our prophets, our sages, our heroes were humanitarians and fighters for individual freedom and justice.

Jewish family pride means, not as many modern rationalists think, arrogance and vanity, but studiousness, intelligence, good manners and good deeds, excellence of character, moral behavior, a tolerant attitude between man and his fellow, justice to the wronged, mercy to the suffering.

When we were dispersed to the four corners of the earth

* Para-adam is Ishmael; Gen. 16:12: "And he will be a wild man."

we took along *Yichut-avot.** Every Jewish family that had
any connection with a learned ancestor passed its genealogy
on from generation to generation. Consciousness of our
family past is a main factor that held us together in the
painful period of exile. While other nations have left behind them only monuments, mummies, and sphinxes, we
have not been swallowed up among the nations. We can
muster evidence of the enormous importance of Jewish
family life in our preservation. Every Jewish home was a
separate bastion of Jewishness, a fortress against assimilation.

Who among us does not remember a Jewish home in the
old country? In the main the family was a whole. The Sabbath, the holidays, the home atmosphere, kept it united. Respect for father and mother, devotion among the children,
even reverence for parents (their word was law), the prayerbook, Jewish love of study, the family around the table
eating not only in order to satisfy the appetite, but to bless
and serve God. All this had a tremendous influence on the
formation of the child's character, keeping him strongly
bound to the family.

The mystic holiness radiated by the Sabbaths and holidays brought comfort, hope, joy, enlightenment, and inter-
dependence. The glory of God actually rested on every Jewish home. The parents were like a resplendent king and
queen. They sang together, discoursed on holy writ, or spoke
on worldly matters with discretion. An idyllic, God-fearing
atmosphere hovered over the table on these days. The house
was filled with spiritual inspiration. It was an armed fortress
which protected us from all the strong winds of Galut life
threatening our existence.

Good manners, a decent attitude to others, devotion to
parents—these must be planted in the child before it stands
on its own feet, even before it can pronounce the words
father and mother. What is Jewish family life and what is the
modern Jewish home? What are the relations between chil-

* Yichut-avot—pride in forefathers.

dren and parents? "Train up a child in the way he should
go, and even when he is old, he will not depart from it"
(Prov. 22:6).

Today's children are reared by mothers who study books
about child upbringing. The mothers, and often the fathers,
become authorities on the most modern methods. They follow the wise counselors who write the books; they have fine,
healthy children, but lacking in good manners, gentleness,
honor, respect of the past. They particularly lack warm love
for their parents and the traditional forms of Jewish family
life.

Honor to father and mother is a life philosophy for Jews
—a way of life. We were the first to proclaim that divine
commandment.

> "In the moment when God said, 'I am your God. Thou
> shalt have no other gods before Me,' the nations of the
> world said, 'God speaks for His own honor.' But when
> he said, 'Honor thy father and thy mother,' they also ac-
> cepted the first commandment."

Even before he could speak and understand, we showed
the child his father's chair, the place at the table forbidden
to the little one. We taught him respect for his grandparents,
for all his family. "Good manners are more important even
than study of Torah," was accepted as the aleph-beth of the
child's schooling. This age-old folkway is not practised in
our day. Today's parents raise their children with every comfort, give them whatever their hearts desire, sometimes more
than they can afford. The children grow up educated, intelligent people with college and university diplomas, but
strangers to their own fathers and mothers. There is a wall
between them and family; the age-long respect for parents
and grandparents is no more. It is shocking to meet learned,
intelligent children who display vulgarity and arrogance in
their behavior to their parents. We meet this attitude towards immigrant parents in children born here; they look
with disdain at those who speak another tongue, or English

with an accent, as though they were come from a strange backward world.

For the most part the fault lies with the parents and the atmosphere they themselves create at home. In order to please their Americanized children they make efforts to adapt themselves to the non-Jewish environment. Whether they succeed or not, and generally they do not (immigrant parents always remain "old-fashioned" to their children), with this aping of the gentile they lose the respect of the young. The home becomes un-Jewish; the bond is weakened; and secular education deepens the abyss. We were taught that learning maketh not a full man; it must be combined with good manners and good deeds. When the parents discover that their children are strangers to them, the break is already too far gone to be repaired. We often hear parents complain, "Our child lacks something." This "something" is hidden from them. It is sensed when their children are grown up, show independence and wilfulness. If they had devoted a fraction of their concern for providing their children with good things, to teaching them the fine old Jewish manners and deeds, concern for other people—the something would not have been lacking.

These can be acquired by the child only from his parents' family life. He must absorb them when still young. Man is not born with good qualities and good practices. Only in the home can these be acquired. Well-bred children are recognized as coming from families where good manners are inbred. Ill-bred children have generally not received such a training.

Children vary greatly in their characters just as do adults. Every child is a creation of his parents, his training, and his family life. Most carry hereditary elements. The fate of man is sealed in his earliest childhood. The behavior of the future member of society is dependent mainly on family conduct for its permanent character.

Educators, psychologists, and sociologists, long recognizing the importance of the family, are studying the virtues and defects whereby men are elevated or debased physically and spiritually.

The Jewish family has become worldly. Its worldliness consists in *tachlit*,* *olam hazeh*,** and mundane pleasures. For the idyllic holiness of Jewish life there is left a vacuum without principles. There are Jewish families wherein the husband or wife, often both, do not want to bear the yoke of family life. They go their separate ways without obligations to each other. The wife is socially taken up, is seldom at home, and leaves the training of the children to outsiders, generally non-Jews; she eats most of her meals in restaurants. The husband, engaged most of the day in business and many evenings socially, has no time to come home to eat.

In these homes family life is loosely knit. There are no close bonds. Husband and wife live under one roof like strangers, with little in common. Seldom does the whole family sit around the table at a meal.

In such circumstances children grow up with a loose relationship, without bonds linking them to their parents. No true love exists between them. All is prosaic, matter-of-fact, materialistic. Children may love their parents because they provide for their comforts, but there is no basic attachment from within. Children of such families could just as readily adapt themselves into any home. That is why there is such a disrespectful attitude. That is why there are so many bad children. Aside from physical proximity there is nothing that ties the child to the parents. Spiritually, mentally, and emotionally they have no connecting link.

These children know almost nothing of Jewishness. If they are at all sentimentally inclined, they may feel that "something" is missing; and they become good material for missionaries. If a missionary speaks to them with glowing eyes about the morality and beauty of Christianity, and there is no substance with which to resist persuasion, they become candidates for conversion.

* Tachlit—worldly purpose.
** Olam hazeh—this world.

Recently we had to deal with such a case. A young Jewish lad of seventeen came to us. His parents and his home were secular, like so many others. He asked to speak with us privately. We were astonished when the boy, physically well developed, whom we knew as one of the outstanding athletes in town and who had never been interested in Jewish affairs, asked us a number of questions about the Jewish faith. After a few minutes we were amazed to hear his slanders against the Jewish religion and his glorification and praise of Christianity. When we sought to clarify the untruth and injustice of his slanders, he demanded to see the sources. He left us not quite satisfied, but with intent to return for further study of religious problems.

From his frequent meetings and discussions we noticed that the boy was reading his questions from a written document. After a frank exchange he remarked that while lecturing on sports to a group of children at the Y.M.C.A., he had become acquainted with a missionary just returned from India. This man filled his head with the cheapness of Judaism and the richness and beauty of Christianity. For weeks the young athlete came to us with his prepared questions from the missionary and noted down our answers. In this way an exchange went on between us and the missionary.

One Sabbath morning the boy came with a New Testament just as we returned from the synagogue. He asked to have a chat with us, and we asked him to wait till after our noonday meal. As on every Sabbath, we chatted, sang the Sabbath zemiroth, and recited grace. The boy watched all this with attention. When we finished and were ready to resume our conversation, he asked, "How often do you do this at home?" I replied that we ate together almost always. On Sabbath and festivals the Jewish religion required the family to dine together in harmony and joy. "Do you always sing these songs in such an intimate family atmosphere?" "Every Sabbath and holiday." "Is this done only by you or do other Jews do likewise?"

When we explained the meaning of the Jewish table, the holiness of Sabbath, the ceremonies of the Jewish holidays and their influence on Jewish family life, there were tears in the boy's eyes. Outside of birthday parties and similar celebrations, he could count on the fingers of one hand the meals which his family had spent with him. Mother and father were always taken up with something else. They ate separately, one not waiting for the other. On Sunday they dined in a restaurant. Strange, cold, and alien. There was no intimacy, no closeness. On Passover, seder night, they ate in a hotel. "I thought," he said, "that all Jews live like that. When I see in a movie a non-Jewish family having a reunion I feel jealous of them. I thought Jews did not do these things. This is the first time in my life I have seen such happiness and intimacy in a family."

This boy is one of thousands of Jewish young people whose attitude to Jewish life is the same, because family life has been emptied of its content and the Jewish attachment to the past has been uprooted. Parents have not taken over the spiritual inheritance of their forefathers, and their children have nothing to inherit. The laws, the traditions, the manners, and the spirit are no longer practiced. The behavior of many Jewish families is not greatly different from that of non-Jews. The Jewish table, especially on Sabbaths and festivals, upon which the Heavenly Presence used to rest and which provided an atmosphere of mystic holiness, making it a table for the Lord, has now become a table of idolators.

The same life, the same foods, are viewed by the child at the homes of his non-Jewish friends. For this reason the Jewish child sees nothing wrong in admiring the background of his non-Jewish playmates. Their social and family life is identical, and the Jewish child becomes embittered against parents opposed to mixed marriage.

"What is the difference? What is wrong?" they complain to their parents. "I love her. She (or he) is the same as I. Religion? You are not religious and neither are his (or her) parents. That is what you told me. What is all the fuss about?"

It is high time for us to speak openly and frankly about the emptiness, lack of spirituality, and worldliness which dominate Jewish family life. No doubt there are other evils, such as the pursuit of good times, the wearing of expensive clothes, card playing, the derogatory attitude to study, which impel the children toward mixed marriages. When we speak about Jewish continuity it is Jewish family life which must be placed at the summit of the agenda.

For generation after generation the sanctity of Jewish family life was implanted in every Jewish boy and girl. The children were inspired with virtue and modesty. Jewish concepts of family purity were based on the firm moral foundations built up over thousands of years.

The worldly Jewish family has cast off its faith in religious concepts. Father, mother, the children, young and old, cast away the elementary rules of esthetics when they walk about at home and in summer places flaunting nudity without shame. Let us concede that scanty clothes in the summer are natural. But what is natural for the others is unnatural for us. Our existence is based on the principle of a people that "dwell alone," and this particularly affects our family life, which differs widely from that of others. Purity and modesty were always our pride, an attribute of which many nations were envious.

Can we in our wildest imagination picture our parents demonstrating their near nudity in full freedom, in the home and on the beach? This is not only against all Jewish esthetics but in disrespect of all order. The parents have thrown away that which was always characteristic of the Jewish home.

The non-Jewish family is also not what it was. There too, there are vanity, lack of discipline, and feeble attachment to parents. The non-Jewish family has become materialistic. Conferences have been called by doctors, psychiatrists, educators, and sociologists to discuss the general problem of the family. They understand the question, both as regards the present and the future.

Their problem is much easier than ours. The social atmosphere is theirs. Nevertheless they still seek means to secure the health of their family life.

We, however, seem little concerned with this problem, even though we see the Jewish home discarding its virtues for the vulgarity of the streets.

A special conference of Jewish experts should be convened by all existing Jewish women's organizations to study how to recapture the character of the Jewish home. These organizations have become a powerful factor in Jewish life. Who, more than they, know the meaning of Jewish family life, and that without Jewish content the home is lost?

Their membership runs to many thousands. Their activities are mainly concerned with philanthropic work, with funds for maintenance of institutions here and in Israel. True, their work is aimed at strengthening Judaism, but it remains only a philanthropic kind of Judaism. There are women's organizations which have cultural programs and propagate Jewish ideals and principles. But in the main these are watered down and devoid of Jewish spirit. They lack the basic Jewish content and traditions.

In their widely diverse work they have neglected the most important thing—Jewish family life. If the Jewish family does not regain its Jewishness, all these efforts aimed at preservation and continuity are worthless.

These organizations with entry to hundreds of thousands of Jewish women must take on the special job of strengthening Jewish family life. The Jewish woman was recognized even before the giving of the Torah as the major factor in maintenance of the Jewish faith. When Moses was called, God spoke to him, "Thus shalt thou say to the house of Jacob, and tell the children of Israel" (Exodus 19:3). Rashi questions this use of a double term of address. "Why," he wonders, "does God address both the house of Jacob and the children of Israel when both have the same meaning?"

He explains it in this way: the house of Jacob refers to the women of Israel, who are the mainstay of the home, whereas the children of Israel refers to the whole tribe; so that God addressed the women first. The Jewish woman makes the home, and it depends upon her whether family life shall be Jewish or not.

Perpetuation of the Jewish family must become a chief goal of Jewish women's organizations. Much weight must be put on basic religious traditional Jewishness. The family must regain its Jewish appearance, its Jewish characteristics. Who more than the Jewish woman carries the concern for the education of her child, and who lives through tragedy when her son or daughter brings an alien spouse into her home?

Who can bear the weeping and laments of the Jewish mother when she feels with motherly instinct the danger and tragedy a mixed marriage entails for her child and her family?

We are faced with a double task—preservation of our own Jewish life and strengthening of the Jewish State in Israel. Both problems depend on the Jewish family.

Because Jewish morality, purity, ethics are found in the Jewish family, of which our father Abraham was the founder, with characteristics different from those of all other peoples, Jewish family life has remained a pillar of Jewish existence and the prime condition of our survival and renewed vitality.

CHAPTER II

SPIRITUAL BANKRUPTCY OF
THE JEWISH HOME

Slowly and imperceptibly, like cancer cells, the disease of mixed marriage penetrates, consumes, and destroys the Jewish family, and Jewish hope of survival. Rabbis of all trends, as well as Jewish communal leaders, are constantly involved with Jewish ailments, but are afraid to touch the most dangerous infection of all. Until now no responsible Jewish leader has cried out publicly about this great Jewish tragedy, to stir the community from its apathy. The serious consequences of assimilation in Jewish life may become constructive only insofar as we are ready to take a lesson for the present and future. Statistics and case histories are not enough. What is needed is to determine the reasons.

No doubt there are other reasons in addition to those to be mentioned which are responsible for mixed marriages. Our experience dates back many years. We consider the reasons given here as most relevant. Basic is no doubt the disappearance of the Jewish home which for generations was a fortress for Jewish life and for the preservation of Jewish values. What happens today can be described as a process of rapid despiritualization, of de-Judaization. Things of the spirit have ceased to play a role in the Jewish homes of this country. A coarse kind of materialism has taken its place. Jewish parents have cast off all thought of the life eternal (*Chaye Olam*) and have devoted themselves with all their senses to the life of the moment (*Chaye Sha'ah*). The *summum bonum* of most Jewish homes has become material gratification, pleasure and good times. The Jewish home has

14

become spiritually empty. There is no longer any historic Jewish continuity; no point of contact exists between the past, present, and future. There is no respect for Jewish learning, for the "Jewish word," for Jewish knowledge and Jewish wisdom. Nor is there any relationship to Torah, tradition, or Jewish customs and the unique qualities of Jewish life.

It is true that the immigrant generation did not succeed in bringing the Torah from the East European *cheder* and *yeshivah;* nevertheless it managed to retain the warmth of mother's Sabbath candles, father's *kiddush,* and the home atmosphere of the holy Sabbath, the ceremonial of the *seder,* the awesomeness of the New Year and the Day of Atonement. These home memories were for most Jewish immigrants something they brought with them to the new land— their home, their historic roots.

How many Jewish children born here will retain in their memories the sanctity of a Sabbath at home, the mystic holiness of the seder night, and the fearfulness of the Days of Awe?

In the child's upbringing two institutions of learning stand out—the school and the home. The home is more important, since it is the fundament of the child's education. In the school the child receives a general training, acquires subjects which make it possible, if he has the will, to attain a profession. The home has greater dominance, since the behavior, manners, mores of his parents and their relationship to the world about them appear perfectly natural to him and become deeply imbedded in his mind and emotional life. However much the child may learn at school, however skilled the teacher, if the home is antithetic to the school, if the actions of mother and father conflict with what they learn there, the school and teacher exert only a perfunctory and minimal influence.

The home builds the child's intellectual life and forms his character, his mannerisms, his attitude towards people. At the home the child gains good or bad manners. Children respect their home atmosphere. Teachers, psychiatrists, and sociologists have long said that in the main there are no good or bad children; there are good and bad parents.

In a suitable home atmosphere where children are raised with intelligence by responsible parents, they generally grow up into proper adults. Father and mother are the pillars of the home. It is they who shape the child's future life. If the home is un-Jewish, the Talmud Torah can be one of the best, the teacher the most capable, the child's will to learn the strongest; but without Jewish content in the home and with parents who do not practice Jewishness, the child will rarely remain attached to Jewish life. He will be a Jew nominally, but not bound by Jewish deeds, never seen in his parents' household.

What are most Jewish homes today? The traditional Jewish way of life is lacking. It is difficult to find a Jewish home, particularly in smaller communities, which contains a Jewish book, secular or religious. In hundreds of Jewish homes we have sought a Jewish book or Bible; with rare exceptions we have not been able to find any, even in translation. Formerly among Jews the book was a necessity, as a coat is for the body. Even the simple unlettered *am-ha'aretz* (ignoramus) had his own prayerbooks for Sabbath and festivals as well as Bibles and other sacred volumes. Jewish children do not see Hebrew lettering in their home. Some families are ashamed to own a Jewish book. To them it is a symptom of the "old-fashioned," backward Jewish immigrant era. There are those who assure you they are good, loyal, and proud Jews, presidents and trustees of synagogues and temples, active members in national Jewish organizations, contributors to the United Jewish Appeal, to Talmud Torahs and yeshivot. They have dozens of receipts. In their homes, however, there is no sign of a Hebrew or Yiddish book. There you can sense a real spiritual poverty.

These homes are equipped with the most expensive furniture, costly drapes and rugs, and valuable and beautiful gewgaws. But there are no Hebrew letters on the bindings of

the volumes the children see, to establish some familiarity
in their minds with this age-old alphabet. The atmosphere
is spiritually empty. Yet these are the homes in which parents
expect to raise children as Jews, to marry other Jewish sons
and daughters. Most of the day the child spends in the non-
Jewish school, playing and working with his non-Jewish
companions. The home to which the child returns is no different from those of his non-Jewish playmates. Why then
should the child grow up differently? Why should he not
romance and marry one of his non-Jewish friends? The
parents who send their children to Jewish schools "shop" for
Jewish education as though it were a bargain in a store
which sells Jewishness as an item of merchandise. Their attitude is one of deprecation. With a sort of exaggerated love
they argue that the child "is too busy, has no leisure time to
play, will not grow up to be a rabbi, will be a Jew anyway."
There is no feeling of responsibility for future Jewish generations, concern for the continuity of their own Jewish life.
When the child is grown, all these things—Jewish learning,
Jewish history, the Jewish Bible—are completely strange and
unknown. One fine day he or she brings home a non-Jewish
girl or boy. To the parents this is a bolt of lightning, a thun-
derclap. They become hysterical and shout, "You should
do this to us! . . . to your own parents who sacrificed their
lives for your comfort and upbringing?" But spiritually the
child is a stranger to them, unable to understand why his
parents are so inflamed against his fiancée. The child asks,
what is the difference between us? Their home is no different
from ours. Our life and habits are the same—what is all the
fuss about?

We live in a world of materialism. Public education has
this same standard. The main goal and object is acquisition
of social position, material success. The child grows up in a
world where everyone is interested in his health, his games,
his leisure pursuits, his personal success. There is no re-
straint, no prohibition. The ideology of the superficial search
for fun is disseminated through the comic strips, the movies,

radio and television. Most Jewish parents wish the child to learn a good profession, to earn money, and have all the comforts and luxuries life can give. This in itself is not undesirable. In Eastern Europe, where education meant Jewish learning, parents made every effort to have their sons study for the rabbinate. Here this same reverence has impelled Jewish parents in another direction—encouraging the child to become a doctor, a lawyer, an engineer, member of a profession. Jewish children learn all the wisdoms of the world except the wisdom of Israel. They know world history—all except the history of their own people. They study all philosophies but Jewish philosophy. They are versed in the life and creation of many peoples, but not the Jewish people. While concerned with the future and prospects of all nations, they give no thought to their own national future or the Jewish future of their own families.

Parents come to the rabbi wringing their hands in desperation, bewailing their bad luck. "Who would have thought our one and only son would do this thing to us? Try talking to him—perhaps you will be able to do something. We can't bear it. He has made us so unhappy. . . . We have gone through every stage of agony. Financially things were never too well with us, but we always gave our child the best of everything. After all he is our only son, the apple of our eye —he is all our hope and all our life. How happy we were when he won a scholarship at high school and a second one at college! He was so popular for his intelligence, his good manners, his speech, and his gentlemanly behavior.

"Yesterday we were prepared for the great event—his graduation from college with top honors. He had offers from large companies offering him fine career opportunities. You can imagine how thunderstruck we were when our son came to us after the ceremony, in cap and gown, escorting a non-Jewish girl and introducing her to us: 'This is June, my fiancée; I think it's time you all got acquainted.' We were stunned and speechless. We left the scene of celebration. Suddenly all our hopes had been blotted out.

"Afterwards, whenever we started speaking to him we became hysterical and broke down. Please send for him, Rabbi; perhaps you will succeed in explaining to him the tragedy he's causing his parents. He will drive us to the grave. He is smart and understands—he will listen to you."

"Did your beloved and only son receive a Jewish education?" asks the rabbi.

"Who had time for that?" the mother immediately changes her tone with a touch of annoyance. "As a child he was rather delicate. When he was about to become thirteen we engaged a Hebrew teacher who prepared him for *bar mitzvah*. What more could we have done?"

"Do you conduct a Jewish home?"

"What exactly do you mean?" asks the mother impatiently.

"Do you keep kashrut? Do you light candles on Friday evening? Does your husband perform the kiddush? Do you observe the Jewish festivals?"

"I am surprised at you, rabbi. You are a modern, enlightened person. How do you come to ask such things? We are not old-fashioned. But tell me, what has all this got to do with our son's tragedy?"

"It has a lot to do with it," the rabbi answers painfully. "Your boy received no Jewish education. In his parents' home he saw no sign of Jewishness. What is there in your son's upbringing that differs in any way from that of his non-Jewish companions? Why should he not marry one of his gentile girl friends whom he loves? Did he learn or absorb anything in his parents' home which he could not already have known or seen at the home of his non-Jewish girl? Why are you so emotionally upset? What else was to be expected? It is a simple thing which anyone might understand. A farmer would never expect to harvest wheat and fruit in the fall if he hadn't sown in the spring. In your house you planted no seed of Judaism: what other result could you expect?"

"He who tends his fig tree," say our sages, "eats from its fruit." We have lost the key to the Jewish home. The house of Israel has become workaday, humdrum, materialistic, alienated, un-Jewish. The holy of holies, the sacred stronghold which maintained Jewish life, has become a place which houses the costliest treasures, but is quite innocent of Jewish spiritual values and traditions.

Parents and children in modern Jewish homes lead a life monotonous and without inner meaning. The worst that can be imagined is to be compelled to spend an evening within one's own four walls, after the day's business or work. As soon as the evening meal is eaten the family flees the house. There is no interest to bind them together. "Thou shalt build a house and thou shalt dwell not therein" (Deut. 28). This curse has been fulfilled in many Jewish homes.

A home means more than four walls and a roof. One must feel completely *at home* there. It must be bound up with one's future and with the raising of one's children. Everything in a home, the rooms, furniture, dishes, crystal, carpets, is merely "the body." There should be a soul to make its occupants feel at one with each other.

We have seen Jewish homes which are palaces and museums. In these there sit Jews who are strangers in their own houses. They do not live according to their historic customs and traditions, but speak a foreign language, observe alien festivals, go in the ways of others. In their innermost heart there gnaws a yearning for a little touch of home, but they have not the courage to make their dwelling more intimate and Jewish. So they escape and create a "home atmosphere" away from home.

The popular *Oneg Shabbat,* and the custom of holding a third seder, have been introduced by Jewish organizations as surrogates for the home. The countless banquets and dinners are similarly the expression of a longing for Jewish home atmosphere. Nationally-minded Jews who have worked for creation of a homeland for the Jewish people, themselves fail to create a Jewish home for their families within their own walls. The Jewish home has become so cold and uninviting because the Jew who longs for a little warm Jewishness is spiritually homeless.

Jewish festivals which used to bring spiritual vigor and reawakening into the home, were once respected guests, impatiently awaited, making a deep and indelible impression on the mind of the child for his later years. Here these holidays have become humdrum and soulless. All that has remained is the gastronomy—*gefilte* fish, *kneidlach, latkes, hamantashen,* and *kreplach.* When the child grows up he retains some vague notion about certain special dishes, but he has never experienced the authentic flavor of a Jewish festival, observed in the traditional way.

The Jewish home has become an inn with vacant rooms, without a soul, without a character, without a culture. How can one look forward to future Jewish generations, to Jewish continuity and Jewish preservation, from homes like this? New synagogues, temples, and Talmud Torahs are constantly erected. This "real estate Judaism" is growing by leaps and bounds. No one, however, as yet is interested in re-constructing the broken Jewish home.

Our community leaders of all ideological and "denominational" trends have not grasped that the home is the basis of the Jewish future in this country. Do they not understand that by building splendid edifices and temples and teaching institutions, they by no means solve the problem of Jewish survival, and that the only security for the future is always the home?

Do our rabbis—both modern and traditional—not know that the Jewish home will not become more Jewish unless the father and mother begin to conduct themselves Jewishly and bring some degree of Jewish warmth, Jewish sincerity, Jewish traditions, books with Hebrew letters, into their homes? Without this, all the well-meaning resolutions passed at conferences and all remedies proposed for the survival of Jewish life have no meaning at all.

The chase after material happiness, greed for pleasure,

the craze for good times, estrangement from Jewish sanctities and Jewish ideals, have led to the epidemic of mixed
marriage. Jewish parents who want to avoid the curse, "Thy
children shall be given over to an alien nation. Thy eyes shall
see this with pain, but thou shalt be without help" (Deut.
28), must bring into their home the sanctities of the Sabbath
and festivals, kashrut, everything Jewish. Jewish parents
who do not wish their home to be the grave of their families,
who want to leave heirs behind them, who do not want
grandchildren who will say "Grandfather and grandmother
were Jews"—must pay as much attention to the spiritual
heritage of their children as they do to their material future.

The Jewish home must be a place where the Shekhinah
rests, for "Thy house is a house of prayer for all peoples."
The great religious leader and philosopher, Samson Raphael
Hirsch, once said that a Christian believes in his church;
the Jew, however, believes not only in the synagogue or
house of prayer, but primarily in his home. The continuity
of Jewish family life, the survival of the Jewish community,
derives from the Jewish home and the behavior of Jewish
parents. If a home means four walls and fine furniture, ori-
ental rugs, expensive furnishings, a television set, and nothing more, it is not a Jewish home. The Jewish home always
was a stronghold of Jewish life, the *sanctum sanctorum*.
From the walls of the home there shone an ideal light, the
beauty of Jewish customs and manners, and the life of the
people living there.

The epidemic of mixed marriage brings tragedy to Jewish
parents and imperils Jewish life on this continent. The fatal
disease which tears Jewish children from their parents—children who become estranged from their own roots like
branches torn from a tree—the responsibility for all this lies
with the Jewish home which is no longer Jewish.

The prospect of the coming generations, the continuity
of national, religious, and communal Jewish life on this
continent—all these depend on whether the Jewish home

can be rebuilt on these historic Jewish foundations, whether it will again regain its soul, its Jewish sanctities, and whether Jewish grace and warmth will resume their status of a few generations ago.

CHAPTER III

THE JEWISH EDUCATION OF OUR CHILDREN

The problem of child training, how to bring up the Jewish child to carry on the heritage of his ancestors—in short, how to raise him to be a Jew—has always been Jewry's most vital problem.

Child education is based on two elements, the general and the personal. Neither of these are based on abstractions; both are founded on tangible premises. The goal of the school is to educate intelligent, honest, and patriotic citizens. At the same time the child must be prepared for his own struggle for existence. He must be taught to feel and think in the direction of social morals and ethics, to carry his part of society's load. He must be disciplined to think independently, to adjust to varying conditions, and to be able to handle all kinds of situations.

Education is the basic prerequisite for group existence. The past becomes the present and prepares for the future. Education preserves the body and the soul of the nation.

No other nation has prized education so much or sacrificed so much for it as the Jewish people. The schools were always considered the cornerstone of religious, national, and social life. Torah is not transmitted by the mere act of birth. It must be transplanted by deliberate effort in each succeeding generation. A Jew permeated by the Jewish spirit *becomes* what he is; he is not merely born to it. The home and the school play their part; by night and by day, on the street and at home, upon awakening and on retiring—every influence shares in the moulding and shaping process.

The ideal of *Talmud Torah k'neged kulam*—"The study of

24

Torah is above all else"—was created by us. What kind of education must be provided to ensure our historic survival? In the two words *Talmud Torah* our sages designated the curricular system of Jewish studies. This is the complete training which draws its sustenance from historic Judaism and which pursues the "golden path" based on love of Israel and attachment to the land of Israel.

Torah is the Book of books given by God; Talmud, the second spiritual creation by the Jewish sages, which fortified and cemented Jewish life and maintained its existence until today. Torah means more than limited religious instruction, but the Torah of *life* (Torat Chaim), a discipline which embraces all problems of daily life. Torah is the philosophy of eternity. It is man's yearning for higher spheres, the cornerstone of civilization. The Torah embraces biology, history, ethnology, philosophy, hygiene, literature. It implies the study of idealism, tolerance, justice, mercy, devotion, sanctity, heroism—a spiritual heroism which strengthens devotion to one's faith and ideals. Sanctity brings one closer to the Godhead ("Ye shall be holy, for I thy God am holy" Leviticus, 19:2).

The Talmud serves not only as a constitution for our spiritual life, but its lofty ethical and moral teachings have established the true range and depth of the Jewish spirit. Its regulations and prescriptions fashioned a characteristic and unique way of life.

Talmud and Torah form a complete system of study and knowledge: knowledge of how to conduct oneself in the world, of behavior to govern relations between man and man, and of man's higher life. He who separates himself from Torah is like one who cuts himself off from life. Torah is the totality of Jewish life. Israel and the Torah are one.

Talmud Torah education links the passing generations with all that came before. The child learns a verse of the Bible just as his great-grandparents did thousands of years ago. It is a chain connecting past and present, creating unity and wholeness in the Jewish people.

In every country our people's process of adjustment to environment has been difficult and costly. Not to give up our olden way of life has always been our main concern. To this end we have devoted all our energies to education of our children. We built schools and *chadarim*. We gave our children, through their Jewish training, an impenetrable armor against alien temptations and influences.

Nowhere in our history have we enjoyed so much freedom or equality as in Canada and the United States. Neither the government nor the population place obstacles in the way of development of our cultural resources. But it is here that we find parents severing the Jewish cultural legacy. The crisis in Jewish education has become a permanent condition. All talk about progress in Jewish education is to a great extent wishful thinking. The fact is that only 25% of Jewish children of school age receive any kind of Jewish education.

There is an illusion spreading through our communal life that the further one departs from the peculiar forms of Jewish life, the more we yield our observances and adopt the customs of our neighbors—the sooner will they accept us as equals; and the barriers that separate Jew from non-Jew will be broken.

If our communal life is not cured of this inferiority complex of "integration" and "accommodation" to the life of the majority group, our children will grow up as "non-Jews of the Mosaic persuasion" and our people will suffer total spiritual bankruptcy. It is time we took an accounting of ourselves— what are we and what do we want our children to be? Are we only nationalists—another nation among the many on the earth? In that case do we raise our children without religion? Or are we a purely religious group, and do we train our children in religion—and nothing more?

Do we want them to continue the life of our parents or to cut their connection with the Jewish past?

Great numbers of Jewish parents completely neglect their children's spiritual upbringing. Later, when they are faced with the accomplished fact of mixed marriage, the seeds of which they themselves sowed, they evidence intense shock and hysteria.

The Sunday schools, which are included in the statistics of Jewish education, where Bible stories are taught on the pattern of Christian schools, are actually guilty of disseminating ignorance. They deceive thousands of parents who are persuaded that through the Sunday schools they can fulfill their responsibilities and provide their children with a Jewish education.

As for the secularist Yiddish (or even Hebraist) education which is a product of the rationalism of the *Haskalah,* whose teachers have more fear of mentioning God than they have fear of God—where are the products of these schools? What knowledge and obligations have remained with them?

Most products of these Yiddishist secular schools have no sensitivity to Jewish spiritual treasures. They have no moral compass to show them the true Jewish way. One cannot at the same time require a strict knowledge of the Scriptures and teach that they impose no obligations, and that the Scriptures, Mishnah, and Talmud possess no sacred value. There can be no bar mitzvah without *tefillin,* without prayers, with a mere empty ceremony. The Sabbath cannot be idealized when it is nothing more than, and no different from, Sunday. The Ten Commandments and the moral principles of the prophets cannot be sanctified when children are taught that these are man-made and can be man-altered. Thousands of Jewish children have come out of this education with a cold "neutralism" toward Jewish survival. There is no visible difference between their life and the non-Jewish life around them.

We know of cases where Jewish youth and girls raised in a secular environment fell in love with non-Jews, and thus answered their parents' remonstrances: "You are neither religious nor observant. You don't believe in God—either in the Christian or the Jewish God. You taught us that all people are alike. Why should you now oppose our marrying someone we love?"

No matter how high-minded the intentions of their sponsors—and I do not doubt their sincerity—they must admit that the modern secular schools, Yiddishist or Hebraist, have not raised a generation imbued with Jewish spiritual values. To write and speak Yiddish or Hebrew, to read their literature, may instill modernism and universalism, but it will not implant that unshakable idealism which for generations gave us the strength to overcome the trials and persecutions of the ages.

Those who believe in the magical power of Hebrew, that it is the key to Jewish survival and the link between Israel and the diaspora, and that therefore all Jewish teaching must be concentrated on the language, are in error. It is an illusion to think that Hebrew will become the language of all Jews in the world. The facts of life are against it. True, it is our sacred duty to teach and disseminate the Hebrew language. But we must not exaggerate, and call it the main instrument for unification of world Jewry.

From a pedagogic point of view we know that most children who study language and literature or history forget what they have learned a few years after they leave school. Even those who pursue higher academic studies generally forget after getting their diploma. How then can we expect Jewish children who study only to the age of thirteen to retain Hebrew in their later years?

"When I speak of Jewish education," writes David Ben-Gurion, "I mean not only the Hebrew language, though Hebrew is the only key to the treasures of the Hebrew spirit. Jewish education is more than merely learning Hebrew. It means implanting in the child's heart the eternal national and universal Jewish values which bind the child to his sources and his origins."

In a lecture at the twenty-third Zionist Congress in Jerusalem, the late Hayim Greenberg said, "For thousands of years Judaism was the expression of a conflict between the Jewish people and its alien environment, and with itself. It is a drama that extends from Genesis to the end of days. The drama was performed against a religious backdrop and in a religious dress. The Jewish soul reacted and resolved its tensions in a religious form. Both the spiritual energies and the cultural values had a religious character, and were clothed in religious values. In our time it is possible for a Jew to know Hebrew so well as to be familiar with the Hebrew names of every botanical specimen or of every cog and particle of a complex machine, but if this Jew does not appreciate such cultural values as *mitzvah* and *averah, nefesh, kiddush hashem, devekut, teshuvah*—then he is not a Jew.

True, we need a worldly education, but it must be conjoined with the Jewish soul. We cannot be content with only a social tie. Our bond exists only in religion.

A tangible bond between the state of Israel and the Jews of the world, avoiding separate Jewish "tribes," is for life in Israel and in the diaspora to be based on Torah-true traditional Judaism, on Jewish wisdom, morals, and ethics.

"The Torah," writes Dr. Dagobert D. Runes, noted author of philosophical works, "always was and still is the only common link between Jewish individuals, families, and communities in all parts of the world. The Torah is the only book that for generations has bound together Jews from patrician mansions in England, from the ghettoes of New York, the remote dust-ridden corners of Yemen, the squalid mellahs of Morocco, and the universities of Italy."

A Jewish religious education gives the child life content, illumines eternal Jewish truths, reveals Jewish treasures, quickens the child's heart, and warms his soul. It gives him the consciousness that he is part of the historic Jewish people, of a two thousand year old tradition of culture, learning, and moral values.

In the process of attaching the child to his people, says Maurice Samuel, no one stage of the Jewish past may be skipped. Not a link may be overlooked in the chain that reaches from the patriarch Abraham to the modern State of Israel.

Our faith, our religion, our national customs and ceremonies, have been not only the bulwark of our existence, but also our strongest weapons against persecution. All who recognize that Jewish education is the decisive factor in preserving our national heritage in the dispersion must recognize that the national and religious form of training is the only dam to stem the flood of assimilation threatening to engulf the Jewish child.

The flame that maintains the soul of the Jew when his body is destroyed—comes from the sparks of training in his earliest youth. The fate that overtook our people in recent years places a serious responsibility upon us. The loss of one-third of our people meant the destruction of our most creative religious and cultural sources. For this reason we must be realistic and not gamble with the upbringing of our children.

For Jews who are not rooted in the unique Jewish spiritual world their link with Judaism is a very weak one. Even between parents and children a barrier exists if the children's mental and spiritual world is not that of their parents. The common practice of a common religious life binds Jew to Jew, parents to children, family to family, and creates a uniform Jewish life.

Only a religious and national Jewish education is capable of maintaining Jewish unity, and of continuing the glorious Jewish heritage. Only this kind of training can develop the soul of the Jewish child and let him live and think as a Jew, bound to his God and his people. Only by teaching the child Torah and Judaism in their traditional principles can the child's heart and intellect be affected, so that he will be impelled and inspired to remain a Jew for all time.

Our sages placed the child's study of Torah on the messianic level. A youth spent in the study of Torah is regarded as a collective messianic act. "Thou shalt not tamper with my Messiah," says an old talmudic text. This is interpreted as referring to small children under care of a teacher. Jewish education must have a national and religious essence, must be rooted in the rock foundation of Judaism, bound to the traditions, tied to its own people, inspired with our future aspirations, saturated with love of Torah, love of Zion, and love of Israel.

CHAPTER IV

CHANUKAH AND CHRISTMAS

There are two months in the year—Kislev in the Jewish calender, and December in the Gregorian—which fall close together; both, too, are months whose festivals have a religious link with light. Kislev has the Chanukah menorah, December the gayly-decked Christmas tree with its many-colored lights. However, between these holidays there has never existed any further relationship. The Jews celebrate the miracle of the crucible of oil in the time of the Hasmoneans; the Christians celebrate the assigned birthday of the Nazarene.

Historically they have nothing in common. Their lights have no mutual significance; indeed, those that convey spiritual light to one person may bring darkness to another. They reflect the deep religious differences which separate those practising these faiths. Where Chanukah commemorates the victory of the Jewish spirit, the miracle of the subjection of the strong by the weak, the conquest of the many by the few, the stubborn struggle for the preservation and self-determination of the Jewish people and Jewish faith, dedicated to serve the God of Israel on the highest principles of the Torah, prophets, and sages, for non-Jews the celebration of this festival has only academic significance. Chanukah, though long a festival of historic, national, and religious significance, has always been celebrated not as a holy day, but on a workaday level. Aside from the practice of kindling the Chanukah lights for eight evenings it has no festive atmosphere like Passover, Shavuot or Sukkot, nor does the traditional liturgy allot it any special prayer except for the short paragraph *Al ha-*

31

Nissim ("For the Miracles") inserted in the daily morning and evening service, and the repetition of the *Hallel* psalms each morning.

Chanukah is marked by a certain gaiety—by various types of play and jollity, card games, the *dreidl,* dominoes, and the eating of *latkes.* It has no religious ritual, no special ban on certain kinds of activity, or a special sanctity, as is the case with the other Jewish holidays.

It is here in America that Chanukah has risen to the status of a major Jewish festival—greater than Passover, Shavuot, or Sukkot—greater even than Simchat Torah. The reason for this rise in prestige is obvious; it is Chanukah's good fortune to fall in the same month as Christmas. It follows our constant attempt to keep up with the gentile Joneses, not only in our daily activity, but in our religious life. To have the synagogue ape the church both inwardly and outwardly, the rabbi, cantor, and choir must be clothed in churchly vestments. Now Chanukah has become the season of lighting candles to compete with the Christmas tree, and it is the season for distributing gifts, as Christians do for Christmas.

We do not mean in any way to detract from the historical value of any festival. We do want to point out, however, that our attitude to Christian feast days is characteristic of the general adjustment to the environment we live in. This shows clearest of all in our attitude to Christmas; every year through November and December, when the retail stores, radio, television, and press concentrate on spreading the "Christmas spirit," this "Christmas spirit" invades the Jewish home. Many Jewish families prepare for the Christian festival just as their non-Jewish neighbors do. Houses are scrubbed and polished, new clothes are bought, Christmas parties arranged, and in some Jewish homes Christmas trees are erected. Certain rabbis become especially active in December. They conduct a competition at fever-pitch with Christian clergymen, as they glorify Christian love and preach paeans of praise to Christianity. They drown out the Chanukah festival, which coincides in time. If they do mention Chanukah it is to demonstrate what Judaism and Christianity have in common.

During December a certain rabbinical body sponsored a radio program over a wide network of stations which bore the missionary-like title, "The Message of Israel." The rabbi engaged to conduct the program was one who purported to be a "specialist" on Christianity. This rabbi (from St. Louis), together with a New York rabbi (who, incidentally, is head of a traditional Jewish organization), both put themselves in the service of the Christmas campaign. Their theme bore the title, "What Chanukah Means to Christians and What Christmas Means to Jews." The broadcast, which cost the rabbinical institution many thousands of dollars, served to spread the Christmas message into Jewish homes. For reasons of "goodwill to men" a mid-Western Reform rabbi proposed to his congregation that they set up a collective Christmas tree "with all the trimmings" in the temple; and in order to give Christmas a special "Jewish touch," he suggested they arrange an *Oneg* Christmas on the style of an *Oneg Shabbat*, that they sing Christmas carols and perform the Passion Play—the play which in days gone by led to persecutions and pogroms with thousands of Jewish victims.

In former days this was the task of *meshumadim*—Jewish apostates, or missionaries, hired for the purpose of persuading Jews away from their Jewish heritage. Today some rabbis do this under the cloak of "goodwill" and brotherhood. These "rabbis" in Israel may well congratulate themselves. Their pro-Christmas activity brings better results than the work of the officially sponsored missionaries. Their congregants imbibe this doctrine, and observe Christian holy days in near Christian ritual. All too often their children marry Christians and their grandchildren are raised as loyal Christians.

If this apostasy propaganda were limited only to the immediate circles of the missionary-rabbis, it would not be so tragic. As an old historic people we know that in all eras we have had our share of Jewish apostates who for one reason or another—generally a selfish one—have glorified the gods of the strangers. The menace is great, however, when the pro-Christian preacher wraps himself in a Jewish prayer shawl, speaks from the synagogue platform, and calls himself "rabbi." Many Jews not too well versed in their faith take these things as stemming from Jewish religious authorities and leaders in Israel. While under the influence of the "missionary-rabbis" they introduce the Christmas holiday into their homes, and set up Christmas trees in their parlors; but to appease their basic Jewish instincts they kindle the Chanukah candles side by side with the Christmas tree.

One day during the week of Chanukah we were invited to the home of a Jew of our acquaintance, a man active in local Jewish communal affairs; we were speechless when in the living-room we beheld a Christmas tree completely trimmed. When we immediately turned to leave the house, the host asked in naive surprise, "Are you leaving because of the Christmas tree? It's just a bit of nonsense—we took it for the children's sake. They see that the neighbors have a Christmas tree and they want one too." "Do you realize what you're doing?" we asked, bitterly. "You're creating confusion in the children's minds. When they grow up they won't know what they are. This is real idol-worship in a Jewish home." "That's just why we asked you over tonight," smiled the naive father. "We inherited a magnificent Chanukah menorah from our grandfather and we'd like you to light the Chanukah candles."

There is no doubt that the increasing tempo of Christmas activities and the singing of carols in the public schools for weeks before December 25 have a definite influence on the Jewish child. We live in a country with a tradition of separation of church and state, where public schools are maintained by the taxes of all, and where the children are drawn from many denominations. Whether in such a country the teaching of Christianity in the public schools is not a violation of religious freedom—one of the most vital principles of our democracy—we do not aim to discuss here. What we intend to establish is that the Christmas observance has permeated the

Jewish community, and has penetrated the Jewish home—
one of the many causes which lead to assimilation and mixed
marriages.

Every year, when December comes, when street, school,
home, and society are filled with the Christmas spirit, and
Jewish public opinion is stirred up, sees the peril of assimilation through the adoption of Christian customs. The lights
on the Christmas trees in Jewish homes flash a danger signal
and Jewry begins to take stock. When the season passes the
excitement ceases, and the scar created by the tree is overlooked. It must be realized that adoption of the Christmas
cult in the Jewish home did not come suddenly. The minds of
these parents were already primed and saturated with assimilationist concepts. The Christmas tree in the Jewish home
is only a measure of the degree to which the outside environment dominates the home, and demonstrates how deeply the
assimilationist disease has crept into these households. Jewish
parents who find excuses for the tree by pointing to their
children's pleasure ("They see it at their neighbors, let them
have one of their own too") are either frivolous, ignorant, or
have had their heads turned by the non-Jewish majority. Their
home life long ago lost its Jewish content; no truly Jewish
home would have a Christmas tree; it would not occur to the
children to ask for one. A Christmas tree in a Jewish home is
a symptom that the home has cast off its Jewishness; Jewish
customs are no longer practised; the children are being raised
in no faith; the path is being cleared for mixed marriage and
severance from their homes and the House of Israel. When
the Jewish home and its practices and observances are identical with those of a non-Jewish home, what is there to distinguish the Jewish child from his neighbor? What is there to
prevent this child from growing up to marry a non-Jew?

There has been considerable talk lately about a Jewish
religious revival. There has been a perceptible return to the
synagogue and a desire to practise traditional Judaism. When
December comes and one sees Jewish men and women busy
preparing for the Christmas celebration, when one beholds

the Yuletide joy on their faces, the Christmas and New Year parties going on in Jewish homes—even in synagogues and temples—the question comes to mind: what are these religious trends we have observed of late among our people? Will not this kind of Judaism—mixed with two parts of Christmas and New Year—some day lead to a new kind of "Christian Judaism"—a Christianity of "Jewish extraction"? There are already signs of this. The fusing of Christmas with Chanukah, the observance of a common "Judaeo-Christian" festival, is one of these signs. Such occasions in which Jewish and Christian children participate in a religious celebration are preparing the soil for this new hyphenated Christian-Jewish religion.

There are large and small Jewish communities where these joint Chanukah-Christmas projects are carried out—on the exclusive initiative of the Jewish group. The most energetic sponsors and participants are always Jewish. The devices used are often incongruous, bordering on profanation of both religions. Once a Jewish community at one of these celebrations invented a Christmas tree shaped so that its branches gave it the appearance of a Chanukah menorah! Such Jews argue that Christmas on this continent is not the Christmas we knew in Europe—that here it is a national holiday devoid of religious content. This attitude on the part of Jews who arrange joint celebrations for interfaith goodwill, is, we think, capable of arousing ill-will and keen resentment on the part of Christians. Despite the complaint that it has become commercialized, Christmas is still essentially a Christian religious festival; and we have the deepest respect for Christians who observe this festival in their own way with sincerity, dignity, and devotion.

The Christmas tree means a great deal to the Christian child and no doubt contributes considerably to his traditional training. As Jews we can honor our neighbors for the faithful maintenance of their religion; we know that religion has an ennobling influence on the child's training and an immeasurable influence for good on man in general. What personal relationship, however, do Jews have to a Christian holy day?

True Christians do not wish to have Jews observing their religious festivals; it must be repeated that Christmas is a genuine Christian religious festival, and is not, as these "goodwill" Jews argue, a "universal" secular holiday. Many Christians feel that Jewish participation in their Christmas profanes its Christian sanctity. For, after all, do Jews believe in Jesus of Nazareth? If not, how do they come to celebrate his birthday? Do Christians celebrate the Chanukah of the Jews?

Furthermore, as if Christmas-Chanukah were not enough, a new fashion has now been set—the joint celebration of Easter and the Jewish freedom festival of Passover. Certain rabbis arrange a model seder in a church attended by Jewish and non-Jewish children. In the presence of Christian clergymen and their congregants, the rabbi solemnizes the tragicomic spectacle—a Christian child asks the Four Questions and the rabbi reads the Haggadah. What impels these missionary-like rabbis to take one of our most sacred rituals and celebrate it in a church? Their answer is "goodwill," brotherhood, interfaith, the improvement of Jewish-Christian relations. Even if this be their real purpose, these joint celebrations are more likely to arouse the very opposite of interfaith goodwill. Every holy day created by a religion is its own; religious ceremonies and celebrations are the private concern of the respective religion and belong exclusively to the inner life of that faith. The fact that they are not shared with other groups has nothing to do with either goodwill or ill-will. Each should cleave to his own religion and to his own God. Those who think that bringing Jewish children to a church and Christian children into a synagogue or jointly observing religious holiday celebrations will bring the Christian majority closer to Judaism are either naive or wilfully blind.

Must it not occur to serious and intelligent Christians that when Jews celebrate Christian festivals, their actions betray a certain emptiness and supine subservience to the majority? Do they not see in this unsolicited intrusion into their faith by non-believing strangers, a profanation of their religious feeling, a total absence of dignity, an obsequious genuflexion to the prevailing environment, and a basic disrespect of, and insincerity toward, both religions? Certainly a continuous and active goodwill program should be carried on to cement friendship between Christian and Jew. Surely, however, this ought to be on the basis of economic, social, and philanthropic relations, and not in the area of religion. Christians do not ask us to sacrifice our religious convictions as the price for interfaith brotherhood; indeed, most Christians, both clergy and layman, have respect for the Jewish religion. It is the "missionary"-rabbis and the "panic-Jews," unhappy with their own Jewishness—for which they find no place in their souls and which they seek to eliminate—who think they can succeed in reducing and minimizing this residue of Jewishness by close and complete association with their Christian neighbors, observing Christian holy days and hoping thereby to find approval in Christian eyes. Such Jews are much more influenced by Christian sermons than Christians by Jewish talks. The Jews involved in this one-sided goodwill movement devote so much energy and enthusiasm to it that they give the impression of willingness to liquidate entirely whatever remaining Judaism they possess, and step across the line that separates them from Christianity, to help fulfill the cause of religious understanding for all time to come.

Rarely in history have the Jewish people had missionary ambitions, and certainly our Christian neighbors have never for a moment had the slightest thought of Judaizing their religion. The proper interpretation of goodwill is that each religious group is entitled to carry on according to its own belief, and that each must treat the other with the fullest measure of tolerance and respect. The war of the Hasmoneans was the first struggle for religious freedom in the history of the world. Whatever religious freedom exists in the democratic countries today owes its inspiration to the days of the Hasmoneans, when the light of freedom for all peoples and all times was first kindled by the Maccabean uprising. The Chanukah festival, therefore, means much more than the victory of the small Jewish nation of that day against the Hellenistic power—it is a triumph of democracy over tyranny and bondage, a victory of faith in the one God over idolatry. But for the victory of the small group of Jewish zealots—the Maccabees and their followers—not only would there have been no Jewish people but the man of Nazareth would not have been born. There would have been no Christianity and no monotheistic religion in the world today. Antiochus' campaign against the Jews had as its goal the removal of the one God of the Jews from His throne, to be replaced by Jupiter-Zeus. Judah the Maccabee and his followers fought the fight for all mankind. Their victory was mankind's victory. The Christian clergy know this well, but, nevertheless, they do not call upon their congregations to observe the holidays of the Maccabees for reasons of goodwill, nor do we ask it of them. We must also admit that the Christian world does not demand of us that we celebrate its holy days. *We* do it of our own will and on our own initiative; we are uninvited guests at their Christmas and New Year celebrations.

The tragic and disastrous thing is that our children invited into the churches by the "missionary-rabbis" receive the impression that the Jewish religion is inferior to the Christian; the proof is, "Even the rabbi glorifies Christianity!" How can this youth grow up in Judaism? Why should he reject intermarriage? Why should children of these mixed marriages in turn not raise their children as Christians? An intensive educational campaign should be conducted every year during the month of December against the joint Christian-Chanukah celebrations. It must be demonstrated to Jewish parents, if they do not understand it, that by bringing the Christmas tree into their homes—despite the innocence of their intentions—they are implanting an alien creed in the heart of their children, who later will deny the God of their fathers and will cut themselves off from Jewish family life. Jewish public opinion must take a firm stand against the Jewish initiators of the Christmas-Chanukah celebrations, who deserve condemnation for their obsequious and undignified assimilationist behavior—behavior which leads to the breakup of the fundamentals of Judaism and endangers our historical continuity.

There is no spontaneous goodwill and understanding when an overwhelming Christian majority share Chanukah and Christmas with Jewish children. The whole idea stems from the Jewish purveyors of assimilationism, who will go to any length to conduct these joint observances. The Christians have at no time evinced any real enthusiasm for these events. Their attitude is one of indifference; if the weaker minority wishes to seek some warmth from their Christmas tree lights, they are quite willing to oblige. These "goodwill" Jews, many of whom occupy prominent positions in our national philanthropic organizations, are responsible for introducing Jewish children to Christian rituals and ceremonies, and eventually can be held responsible for the estrangement of the children from their ancestral faith. Jewish parents who erect a Christmas tree in their homes on the pretext, "They see it at their neighbors; let them have one to play with at home," are profaning their faith, and lighting their children's way to the Church. Their behavior is even more destructive when they kindle the Chanukah menorah next to the Christmas tree; when they do this they degrade the Chanukah festival, turning it into an auxiliary ceremony in celebration of Christmas.

To those rabbis who wait impatiently for the Christian festive season as though it were a Jewish holiday—men who are heads of organizations—to them must be put the question asked by Elijah of the prophets of Baal: "How long halt ye between two opinions? If the Lord be God, follow Him; but if Baal, follow him!" (Kings 18). This was the reaction of Jewish opinion to one of our best known Reform rabbis, an ardent Zionist and a veteran fighter for Jewish causes and civil rights. One December, when he delivered a Christmas sermon calling upon Jews to recognize "Christ," a storm broke upon him, and despite his achievements for his people, Jewish opinion was outraged. Eventually he regretted his Christian sermon, asked forgiveness, and openly admitted his error. In his later goodwill speeches the same rabbi declared to Christian audiences that goodwill does not mean that each faith must depart from any of its cardinal principles; each must proceed along its own tried and tested ways.

We have much in common with the Christian world. We are linked with it politically, economically, socially, philanthropically, and even culturally; a religious link, however, is not part of the program expected from us by Christian neighbors. As a minority we have full right to the maintenance and practice of our religious differences. Only those Jews who have lost all semblance of their historical consciousness and suffer from an inferiority complex can adopt the utterly unfair concept that the minority must give way to the majority because the latter is large and strong. This is the very opposite of the meaning of our Chanukah festival; it is not adjustment to the environment, but self-negation and capitulation. In any religious partnership with the majority, we are the losers; they reap the profit and we the loss.

In our effort for group survival in these countries of the West, we must fight without compromise against any profanation of our Chanukah festival which would link it with the Christmas celebration; we must see that Jewish children be raised as Jews, and Christian children as Christians. As said, we have great respect for the Christian faith, its festivals and rites, but this does not mean we must adopt a ritual which our own religion forbids. There is ample beauty and grace in Chanukah to inspire our children and illuminate our ideals. Reality and legend, heroism and bravery, are united in Chanukah, making it one of our finest celebrations, the story of our willingness to sacrifice even life itself for our Torah and our God. Chanukah can be an educational motivation: its tales and legends can awaken love of and pride in our Jewish heroes. The parents must make the Chanukah observance so impressive that the children will remember it from year to year, and transmit its glories to their own descendants.

Just as Mattathias and his sons declared open war against the Greeks and the Hellenistic assimilationists who were ready to give up their own spiritual heritage to be absorbed by the majority, so must we war against the missionary-rabbis and the enslaved, sycophantic, cringing Jews who every year are involved in their mixed Chanukah-Christmas celebrations. These lead Jewish children to the Church, to mixed marriage, to the ultimate extinction of the Chanukah lights, to decline of our Jewish way of life, and finally, to annihilation of Judaism itself.

CHAPTER V

THE "INTEGRATION" PERIL

"Integration"—a new word in our vocabulary in place of
the old word "assimilation"—has acquired a position in Jewish
life on this continent. "Integration" means that Jewish life
should adjust itself to the surrounding non-Jewish environment. If Jews are not willing to lose or deny their identity,
they must nevertheless become an *integrated* part of general
American life. Jewishness and Americanism need not contra-
dict each other. One must be an American or Canadian in no
less degree than a Jew. Religion, of course, remains purely a
personal matter.

The propagators of this integration ideal are actually more
dangerous than those who preach open assimilation. The old
word *assimilation* always contained within itself a sound of
warning, of self-negation, even of apostasy. The new word,
however, is misleading and deceptive. It can delude innocent
and well-meaning Jews who would normally turn with revulsion from "assimilation."

Integration, whose purpose is to adjust and fit Jewish life
to surrounding society, has the effect of patterning our own
internal Jewish life on this non-Jewish model. It eliminates
barriers, ideas, principles, and practices which over many generations have created Jewish life as we know it in all its color
and spiritual depth. It is the open door to assimilation and
mixed marriage.

The old assimilationist slogan of the *Haskalah,* "Be a Jew
at home and a human being (*mensch*) outside," is the direct
ancestor of the theory of the integrationists. Experience has

43

proved long since that this slogan led to total assimilation and apostasy.

No variety of complete integration exists which can in any way lead the way to inner integration. Jewish history and Jewish life have taught us countless times the falseness of the idea that the only difference between Jew and non-Jew is one of religion, and that aside from this one distinction they can be alike in their feelings, concepts, and convictions,

The conception that the sole difference is one of religious cult and that beyond this no spiritual distinction exists between the Jewish and the non-Jewish world, turns the Jew into a kind of dual being. In the synagogue he is a Jew with certain obligations to his religion; in secular matters which have no concern with his religion, he is on the same level as the non-Jew.

In actual fact the new idea is not different from the old notion of assimilation, except that the integrationists do not require that the Jew deny his Jewish identity. The results, however, lead to the same path as the Haskalah type of assimilation—intermarriage and the breakup of our characteristic Jewish life.

The argument that integration merely means acclimatization, Americanization, and acculturation makes this theory all the more dangerous. After all, what do acclimatization and acculturation mean, if not that the Jew accept the non-Jewish civilization and culture, and adopt the same outlook on life as the non-Jew, that outside the synagogue he is to behave exactly like his non-Jewish neighbors?

Is this not the old assimilationist inferiority complex of placing the non-Jewish culture and standards higher than our own, of having the Jew learn behavior by slavishly imitating the non-Jew?

We have been affected by a peculiar kind of optical illusion. Wherever we turn we have eyes only for the superiority of non-Jews and for our own inferiority. Even nationally-minded Jews who do not follow the k'chal ha-goyim concept (Israel is a nation like all the others), feel that in the diaspora Jews should be "integrated" with the non-Jewish population, because the differences between the two civilizations are "minute."

This idea is completely false and contrary to the facts of Jewish survival. The difference between Jewish and non-Jewish civilizations is a chasm—an abyss between heaven and earth. For one thing the idea of dividing a person into two parts—Jew and human—is foreign to Judaism. The theory that civilization is one thing and Judaism another, that Judaism connotes religion and that civilization connotes culture and worldliness, is a flat denial of the content and range of Jewish life.

To the Jew, Jewishness and civilization are one and indivisible. The Law of Sinai is the foundation of both Jewish and Christian civilizations. "In the beginning God created" is the start of their thinking and philosophic processes. The word *Elohim* (God) is the focal point of human thought. For the Jew, Judaism is his philosophy which comprises the universe, answers all the questions of heart and soul, and has an answer to all worldly events and problems of society.

The Jewish civilization which is a part of the Jewish religion has standards and values for all of human life, for all that lives on this earth, for all that can be reached by human reason, and for all that human imagination can contain. For the concepts of God, Man, and Nature, Jewish civilization possesses a definite point of view and a well-defined answer. In the matter of man's behavior and ethics, in which there are no two schools which agree and where none has succeeded in showing man a clearly defined way in life, the philosophy of Judaism makes a categorical demand: "Ye shall be holy, for I the Lord thy God am holy" (Leviticus 19:2).

There is a striking contrast between Jewish Torah and civilization and the civilization of the nations. Only an ignoramus would state that they are almost alike, so much alike that Jews can live and express themselves fully in a Christian civilization.

These two can never be matched and never be harnessed

as a single or hyphenated unit. The exponents of a "Judeo-Christian civilization" are outspoken assimilators, whose efforts lead Jews to apostasy and to the collapse of our people's life.

Since the revelation on Mount Sinai, when the Children of Israel received the gift of Jewish civilization from the Creator, they have persisted in declining to accept any other.

Hundreds of thousands of our martyrs have perished because of the contrast between the civilizations, because they were unwilling to give up their religion and way of life for another.

Jewish history from its beginning until today serves as proof that Jewish civilization is a world of its own, separate and apart from the civilization of other nations. Each of these has its own answer to the problems with which the human spirit is concerned and its own approach to and evaluation of God, World, and Man. They have differing concepts of the position and condition of Man on earth.

The differences are particularly sharp in relation to the duties, obligations, and behavior of Man—something the integrationists wish to equate in a sort of spiritual *Gleichschaltung*.

The focal point of the civilization of Judaism is that God and God alone stands over the universe which is His creation. God can never be involved in an earthly physical relationship with humans. Man is a creation of God who must follow God's will. He must not pursue his own wishes and yield to his passions. Not all that Man wants is authoritative. In any conflict arising from Man's impulses he must bend to the will of God and fulfill God's command. Man cannot be his own lawgiver, for not all that Man does is just and good. Truth, righteousness, and justice for Man are ordained by God, and the way of righteousness for Man is to observe and fulfill God's wishes.

The focal point of non-Jewish civilization is Man. The faith of Christian civilization is centered on a man, his birth, his death and resurrection. Man is his own lawgiver. He decides what is right and what is wrong. His passions and demands are therefore the key motivations. There are no injunctions preventing him from carrying out his will other than his own reason, his strong counter-will, or his self-created "laws." His behavior comes not from heaven but from Man. Despite its theology, Christian civilization is humanly based.

The contrast is therefore clear and uncompromising. The difference does not lie, as many think, in dogmas and principles, but it is fundamental, underlying the two *Weltanschauungen* of beliefs, thinking, feeling, and deeds.

The chief duty of Jewish religious civilization is to improve man's deeds. The demands and commands of goodness, justice, and honesty between man and man, are more important in Judaism than the duties of man to God. There is no such thing in Judaism as saving one's soul by belief in someone or something. Each of us will save his soul by practising honesty and not harming his neighbor.

Only the ignorant or those with a latent urge toward assimilation can speak of a "Judeo-Christian civilization." It is a latter-day *ma-yafith*, a slavish self-humiliation before the non-Jewish world, particularly since it is this Christian civilization —one spoken of as the ideal of justice and humanity—which led to the brutal extermination of one third of the Jewish people.

How can Jews "integrate" with a civilization that practises injustice to Jews, a civilization that is not concerned with man's deeds, with what he is, but with his birth and ancestry, which permitted a bestial pursuit of men as though they were vermin, solely because they were born Jews and had a different faith?

The preachers of integration, however, are not concerned with this. They are dazzled by the beauty of the world's culture, overcome by the attraction of assimilation. Their Jewishness is shallow and meagre. They bow to all that is non-Jewish and seek shelter under the protective umbrella of world civilization.

This trend to "May the House of Israel be like that of all

the nations" is an old one. It comes from inner weakness, lack of confidence in one's own strength and resources, from self-hatred and a drive to escape, from deprecating the heritage which flows in one's veins, chiefly from reluctance to carry on the fight for our historic mode of life.

The integration sickness has eaten into the body of Jewish life and the results are now perceptible. Walls which for generations stood between Jew and non-Jew have been razed. The Jewish Sabbath has been replaced for many by Sunday. Kashrut, regarded as a product of the ghetto, has been cast aside. Jewish festivals are antiquated institutions. Jewish education has been dropped to the minimal level, the Jewish folk-tongue condemned to decline. "Goodwill" and "brotherhood" have become the ideals and activities of national, even religious, Jewish organizations. Jewish charitable establishments point with pride to their "non-sectarian" character. Rabbis and Christian clergymen fraternize and exchange pulpits, and as Dr. Oscar Handlin, professor of history at Harvard, said at the National Conference of Jewish Social Work in Atlantic City: "In its external appearance Judaism is beginning to resemble a Protestant denomination, the synagogue a church, and the rabbi a Christian clergyman."

The danger of integration is even greater in that its advocates argue that their ideal is really to adjust Jewish life to general American life, implying that whoever opposes their idea is against the Americanization of the Jews. Their line of reasoning is quite false and their "Americanism" is opposed to the concepts of the founders of the American republic. The Pilgrim Fathers who came to the New World after bitter experiences and painful wanderings were men greatly inspired by the Law of Moses and the divine commandments. Many of the creators of the American Constitution regulated their communities according to the precepts of the Law of Israel. The first book they published was an English translation of the Psalms for instruction of their children (most of whom, incidentally, bore biblical names). There were clergymen (and laymen too) in those days who propagated the idea that

Hebrew, the language of the prophets, should become the official tongue of the new republic. On the Freedom Bell of the United States—that rang out the nation's independence—they inscribed the words from Leviticus 25: "And ye shall proclaim liberty throughout the land, unto all the inhabitants thereof."

The father of the republic, George Washington, spoke of the Jews of his day as "Children of Abraham's seed." He expressed the hope that the people of America would enjoy the earthly and spiritual blessings of the God of Israel. What we call Americanism is actually an off-shoot of Jewish spiritual roots which fed and nourished the roots of American life.

This was the attitude of the founding fathers of the American republic. It occurred to no one at that time to demand from the Jews of America adjustment to "American" conditions, or that they declare themselves Americans of the Jewish faith. The fact is that the whole idea of adjusting Jewish life to so-called American spirit is itself far from the American spirit. It is a rather cheap import from Western Europe, where the negators of their Jewish origin debased themselves, their religion, and national feeling in order to find favor with the non-Jewish population. What this attitude led to is well known to us—mixed marriage and apostasy.

Integration is worse than assimilation, for its exponents convince themselves and others that their intention is to improve Jewish life. In this way they confuse the minds of the Jewish masses and win adherents.

The argument that integration proposes to Americanize our Jewish life is utterly false. On the contrary it is an imitation of what has happened with other immigrant groups. These immigrants took Americanism to mean the shedding of all their native cultural heritage. For Jews, however, this was never necessary, for it is through Judaism that true Americanism can find its most appropriate expression. Americanism was rooted in the principles of Judaism. Jewish life and Jewish behavior do not need to Americanize themselves.

The integrationists suffer from an old mental ailment. They

have persuaded themselves and seek to persuade others that it is because of our differences, our peculiarity, that we are disliked by the non-Jewish world. The moment we alter our way of life to conform to that of the environment, prejudice and discrimination will vanish.

This idea is as old as the Jewish exile. In every epoch there were Jews who suffered from this complex and who preached integration and religious cooperation. In every case the result was a bitter disappointment. The children married out of the faith and were lost to the community of Israel; the outside world, however, still regarded them as Jews.

In our own days we have seen at close hand the deep tragedy of this distortion. The greatest adjustment ever made to the non-Jewish environment was that which for many decades was practised by the Jewry of Germany. German Jews, because of this *Gleichschaltung* to German culture and life, gave up their Jewish nationality and coined the phrase "German citizens of the Mosaic persuasion." When Hitler came to power, he unearthed the old communal records and exposed more than a million apostates and their progeny, whose conduct and manner of life were more German than that of the "Aryan" Germans. They did not escape the fate of the Jews. Together with European Jewry they too were deported to the concentration camps, and along with the others they were tortured and gassed in the German crematoria.

But the integrationists will not learn from the past. The truth is that blind and gratuitous hatred of Jews never made any distinction between religious or non-religious Jews or between those who do or do not openly practise their faith. Non-Jews free of anti-Semitic bias never demand any religious adjustment of us or any kind of religious partnership. They are content to have our cooperation in all other areas, and maintain the deepest respect for the practices of the observant Jew. To anti-Semites, no amount of cooperation or integration will make any difference. In fact, their hatred becomes even greater when Jews seek to imitate them by a "protective coloring" or by denying their individuality, and to penetrate into non-Jewish clubs and society.

The integrationists do not ask the Jew to deny his Jewish identity. On the contrary they say that in contact with the non-Jews, we are to appear as Jews. It is only that our conduct and appearance and general aspect should so approximate those of the non-Jews—should be so devoid of Jewish content tradition, Jewish tradition, and Jewish peculiarity—that the non-Jews will not know what distinguishes them from us. The *maskilim* of a previous generation, when they held forth the slogan "A Jew at home, a man of the world abroad," at least reserved the home for Jewishness. Later they realized their fallacy. They saw that if one is not harmoniously at one as a Jew—abroad as well as at home—the non-Jewish street will engulf the Jewish home. Our integrationists long ago opened the Jewish home to outer influences, with the result that there is nothing left to preserve or maintain. What partition then will separate the Jew from the non-Jew?

Despite its paradoxes the integration idea has seized hold even of important segments of Orthodoxy—a sector which should be worlds apart from it. Certain elements seek to adjust their Jewishness "to appease the non-Jew." Strange as it seems, it is nonetheless a fact that many orthodox Jewish circles follow the point of view of the integrationists, writing off important parts of traditional Judaism with a view to conforming to the non-Jewish milieu, the pretext being that this creates better interfaith relations.

Certain orthodox Jewish circles have even recently begun to follow the Reform movement in creating an "easy" Judaism. An extraordinary phenomenon—"easy for the children" —specifically, deleting any peculiarities and special characteristics which set our children apart from the environment.

The assimilationism propagated under this illusory name has captured large masses of Jews. It leads to throwing off the yoke of Jewishness, as well as concern and responsibility for the Jewish future. Because of this idea of adjusting Jewish life to the world around us, the widespread mixed marriage evil can be seen in clearer perspective. It is due not so much to malice or animosity as to the shattered barriers. Jewish children simply know very little Judaism and practise even less. Judaism, as far as they understand it, is no obstacle in their path to intermarriage.

And here lies its danger. It extinguishes the spark of faith in one's own religion and in the peculiarly Jewish way of life. The whole way of Jewish life becomes a sort of museum relic which has no place in modern Jewry.

This new orientation under the name of integration must be fought with all our resources. Because of its illusory appeal it is much more dangerous than the assimilationism of a previous day. Its exponents must not be allowed to deceive themselves or others into saying that Jews are a people like all others, that Judaism has qualities similar to other faiths, and therefore Jews ought to adjust their lives and behavior patterns and integrate them into non-Jewish life. The world knows that we are different, and we will not and must not give up that difference.

It is as old as the Jewish people. It began when Abraham first conceived the distinction between idolatry and monotheism, and it has existed in an unbroken line since then. It is one of the bases for the external hatred towards us, and it is the best guarantee for our survival. For it is an accepted historical axiom that the group whose members show a determination to stay as they are, different from others, will have a secured existence.

We are a people divinely ordained to be a minority forever; in the words of Deuteronomy 7:7, "for ye are the fewest of all peoples." We always bore this knowledge with pride and dignity. Our existence as a minority for a period of 2000 years is an achievement without parallel in history. Thanks to our religion and our different and peculiar way of life we built up the mighty fortification against the outside world which so often tried to penetrate our inner Jewish life and destroy it.

Years of exile eroded our peculiarity. Nations tried with all their might to root out our specific differences, to influence our life, to imprint their model upon us; but this never succeeded, for in all times and in all generations, the Jew felt that thanks to his difference ("and their ways of worship are diverse from all people"—Esther 3:8) he owes his existence, and it is through his distinctive way of life that the Jew has something to contribute to world civilization and to mankind.

This way of life is what the Jew accepted when he received the highest gift of the Divine—the Book of books—the Torah. This different way of life created Jewish prophecy, developed the urge to sanctity, spiritually enriched his own life, and made possible the Jew's inestimable contribution to the treasury of human creativity, the human spirit, and civilization.

It is the quintessence, the foundation of all foundations, in the Jewish religion and in the security and survival of the Jewish people.

CHAPTER VI

THE PROBLEM OF JEWISH YOUTH

(*Ignorance, Assimilation, and Mixed Marriages*)

The Bible, except for Moses, devotes its greatest attention to the personality of Jacob. Of the three great forefathers—Abraham, Isaac, and Jacob—the last was faced with the greatest perils, endured the harshest pain, overcame most obstacles. Jacob's career was filled with risk and struggle. By dint of his inexhaustible energy, the Torah tells us, did he build the House of Jacob. As a loyal and faithful father, he presided over his family, from which was to arise the people of Israel. It was Jacob who first commanded the fight against idolatry, abandonment of alien ways of life, faith in their ancestors' God, service to Him only.

> "Then Jacob said unto his household, and to all that were with him: 'Put away the strange gods that are among you, and purify yourselves, and change your garments; and let us arise, and go up to Beth-El; and I will make there an altar unto God, who answered me in the day of my distress, and was with me in the way which I went.' And they gave unto Jacob all the foreign gods which were in their hand, and the rings which were in their ears; and Jacob hid them under the oak which was by Shechem."
>
> (Genesis 35:2–4)

When at last Jacob felt his strength passing from him, and knew that he was soon to die in a strange land, leaving his family in the midst of idol-worshipers, "he looked into the future and trembled" (Midrash Rabbah). He feared that his children or grandchildren would adopt Egyptian customs, merge with the dominant population, and forget their faith in the God for whom he had sacrificed so much. He therefore assembled his sons before his death to speak of their future.

"Bury me not in Egypt. Remember the God of Israel. Wherever you may be and whatever may happen to you, remain faithful heirs of your ancestors' divine ideal."

When Jacob, father of the Jewish people, looked into the distant future and saw the perils of assimilation, the impulse to be submerged in the environment, he trembled for the security of his posterity.

It would be trite to say that the future and existence of any nation depend upon its youth. This truism applies with particular force to the Jews.

Among other nations, when children do not follow the same path of life as their parents one factor remains constant—they are still children of the same nation. There is no danger that a change in habits by the youth will cause the nation to lose its identity, or expose it to extinction. It is different with Jewish youth. When Jewish youth turns away from the ways of the elders and adopts non-Jewish ways, absorbing other people's habits, cultures, and languages, marrying their sons and daughters, it gives up its Jewish identity. The young become assimilated and in time disappear entirely from the Jewish community.

No other subject is discussed at our various conferences in as much detail as the problem of youth. All efforts to solve it notwithstanding, Jewish youth today stands at the crossroads, lost between two worlds, not knowing in which direction to turn. The young Jewish generation has deviated from the old path trodden by its parents, yet feels alien on the threshold of the non-Jewish world.

Most of our Jewish young today have been raised without an interest in Jewish life, without the stimulation of Jewish idealism, without an awareness of their historic ties with the past. Despite all analyses and treatises, no Jewish youth movement has yet been created which has proven able to prepare the future generation for a creative national and religious Jewish life.

There are Jewish young people who do not want to be identified with Jews at all, and who say quite openly that they have released themselves from their Jewishness, as an obstacle to their complete Americanization.

A survey carried out by the noted social psychologist, the late Kurt Lewin, revealed that among Jewish young men and women there is an increasing desire to be closer to non-Jewish society, to be more and more like the surrounding majority. Even sadder is a tendency among adult Jewish youth to attribute to Jews all sorts of defects and faults bruited about by overt and dissembling anti-Semites. A large proportion of those queried complained that Jews were "noisy," "bad-mannered," "speakers with their hands," "unpunctual at appointments." In general they referred to alleged Jewish failings as axiomatic certainties. When asked about good qualities in Jews, few of those interviewed had positive comments to make. Historic Jewish practices, Jewish religious ideas and customs, were looked upon as obsolete, and distasteful in comparison with the life of the non-Jew.

The survey also revealed that the younger the Jewish child, the more positive its attitude to Jews and Judaism. In the course of time their interest cools and they develop contrary attitudes.

All through Jewish history our home and family life has been our great pride, for which others envied us. These were the fortresses that helped sustain us. There was a strong link between parent and child. Seldom was the Fifth Commandment violated. Grandchildren were raised to have the greatest respect for their parents' parents. The youth did not look with disparagement on their elders. When children married and the family grew, the family circle expanded and yet drew closer.

True, then too there were differences of opinion between parents and children. But even when sons made some heretical remark about their parents' beliefs, they nonetheless retained a reverence for their parents' *Weltanschauung*. The differences were mainly of the mind. Deep in their hearts there was love and understanding between parents and children—a relationship now vanishing.

The love, mixed with awe, for the patriarchal father-image is gone. The parents are no longer masters in the Jewish home—it is the children who rule. Because of the new pseudo-scientific concepts about the child's psyche (too strict a parental discipline will do it irreparable damage) the father has lost his influence. He is the breadwinner and provider of necessities, nothing more. He rarely has much to say about his children's education and conduct.

This applies not only to immigrant parents and their native children, but equally to parents born here, and their children. They may be, and often are, fine children. But their education creates a barrier which renders their elders backward, retarded old folks who should be honored only on Mothers' or Fathers' Day.

Much of the responsibility, as we have shown, is borne by the home devoid of Jewish spiritual values. There is no sense of the holiness that for generations pervaded Jewish family life, when all would meet around the table on Sabbaths or festivals to pay homage to parents. No longer do they feel the awe and solemnity of the holidays—impressions that stayed with the child all his life. Our children have the best manners, are familiar with all the rules of etiquette and social relations, show tolerance and respect for all. To their own parents, however, they are cold.

Many parents live lonely, isolated lives after their offspring marry. There is nothing worse than estrangement from children. They raise and nurture them in all their care and love, but when the children grow up a chasm opens between them across which no bridge has been thrown. The parents feel orphaned and rejected when they recognize this unbridged gap.

Differences between succeeding generations have always existed. It is normal that there be divergent attitudes and behavior pattern between old and young. It is said that prior to the coming of the Messiah Elijah would appear:

> "And he shall turn the heart of the fathers to the children, and the heart of the children to their fathers."
>
> (Malachi 4:6)

Never before, however, has there been the distance between the generations that exists today, two entirely different worlds without any link or tie.

The child need no longer obey the parent, but the parent must "adjust" to the life and ideas of the child.

Not only do sons and daughters of advanced education feel they have a better understanding than their parents, but as soon as he leaves primary school the child develops an attitude of disparagement and of revolt.

When the commandment "Honor thy father and thy mother" no longer is heeded, and children take no cognizance of their parents' feelings, and when the future of their family group is no longer a matter of concern to them, it follows naturally that a Jew falling in love with a young man or woman of another faith, will give no thought to the question of whether that conduct will please the parents.

Love has become the idol, the fetish which every "modern" youth must serve. Everything and everyone that stands in its way must be sacrificed. In the ardor of his passion the youth gives no thought to his parents, to the suffering and pain caused them. These young people are "modern," mature enough to know what is best for their own interest, and advanced enough not to waste consideration on the superannuated concepts of their elders, who have not adjusted to the times.

In general, youth today—non-Jewish as well as Jewish—is being raised without ideals. The main goal is to attain material success. Career, wealth, and good times are taken for granted, as proper aims. It is rare to find a young person who is ready to dedicate himself entirely to an ideal of any sort. The trend to professions is not based on intrinsic interest in science or knowledge, but on the material advantage to be gained.

The ambition to give children a higher education is common to all parents, rich or poor. Parents who extend themselves beyond their resources to pay for their children's education do so on the ground that they want something for their young they themselves did not get, that will spare them their own economic struggle.

Educators and sociologists have stated that universities are not the place where a person receives his basic education. The home and parents are the main factor. The university cannot shape the character and qualities of the student if the student does not bring these from his home. We ought not measure a graduate by his university degree. We have known experts in their professions who demonstrated little in the way of personality, character, or intelligence. Parents who strain to send their children to the university are not necessarily doing them a favor. Sometimes they do themselves a disfavor.

As critical as one may be of students as a whole, it must be said that, even in the circles of academic careerism, exceptions exist. There are many students who are ripe for Jewish moral and spiritual influence in Yiddish or Hebrew, but there is a serious language barrier. The Jewish periodical press, published in English, cannot be the full source of intellectual or spiritual inspiration. Most Anglo-Jewish publications seem to deal with a restricted number of subjects. The frequent treatment of the theological differences between Orthodoxy, Conservatism, and Reform may give the impression that its readers are embroiled in religious disputation. Actually all is peace in the religious field. Most members belong to a congregation not out of conviction or religious principle, but because of friendship, social milieu, or practical convenience. Those who can afford it frequently belong to synagogues of all three "Judaisms."

Despite the talk one hears about the revival of religion among Jewish youth, which seems to be based on the construction of new synagogues and temples, this so-called revival is superficial and illusory. There is no real religious awakening and no deepening of the spiritual impulse.

People who have no idea of Sabbath observance and who are far from Jewish rituals, declare themselves "orthodox." Women who do not practise Judaism in their homes profess to be "religious" and presume to speak with authority on "Judaism." Most of those who predict a glorious future for Judaism and Jewish education, send their own children to a Sunday school.

We do not deny that there has taken place some partial re-awakening among American Jewish youth. The majority, however, is still indifferent to Jewish spiritual values. At best some have a rather diffuse, nebulous sentiment about being Jewish—a feeling without body or permanence. Ignorance of things Jewish is still increasing.

There are thousands of Jewish youth who know absolutely nothing of Hebrew literature, and thousands of men and women with university degrees who do not know one letter of the Hebrew alphabet from the other.

Most lack a basic Jewish education. Their spiritual equipment consists generally of what they can recall of the bar mitzvah party and speech. About Jewish festivals they have a confused notion of matzah, matzah-balls, the Chanukah rattle, Hamantashen, blintzes, and kreplach. But they have no idea of historical and symbolic significances. The practices and customs identified with our national and religious development are unknown. They know very little Jewish history; they have no organic link with the joys or sufferings of their own people, and the 2,000 year Jewish dispersion. The bloody events of our long martyrdom are totally unfamiliar to them. They are unaware of the tortures, slaughters, blood libels, inquisitions, and auto-da-fés of the Christian world against their innocent forefathers, whose only sin was to be Jews and to believe in the God of Israel.

In the colleges and universities they attend, Jewish young

people learn to glorify the cultures of other nations, deify non-Jewish heroes, idealize non-Jewish literatures and languages. They do not learn of the Jewish sages, and heroes who placed their impress on the civilization and the life of the Jewish people, and of the world.

Thousands of young people come in contact with Jews and Jewishness in our colleges through the Hillel Foundations sponsored by B'nai Brith. These future doctors, lawyers, engineers, chemists, journalists, and researchers whose academic studies are on an advanced level are exposed to a most elementary level of Jewish knowledge in a rather casual manner, through the Foundations. This "basic Judaism" is not rooted deeply and cannot turn the students into Jewish scholars. Moreover, scholarly Jews and Jewish scholars are two separate concepts. Being born of Jewish parents and having attained social advancement by no means indicates a position of respect within Jewry. A famous scholar of Jewish birth who has never played an active role in Jewish life, is not a *Jewish* scholar. A Jewish scholar is one whose scholarship is placed at the service of his people. It is a sad fact that most Jewish-born secular celebrities have no desire to be identified with their origin. Many suffer from a psychopathic hatred of their own relatives.

A considerable part of educated Jewish youth suffers from this inferiority complex, deeply ingrained. Their Jewish sensibilities are almost completely eroded by assimilation. They hate themselves for what they are.

Since the others know they are different, they find satisfaction in behaving and talking as though they are not what they are. More than anything they hate themselves for being what they do not wish to be. They do not grasp that this is their own incurable tragedy, that it is impossible to get out of one's own skin. One cannot be other than what one is.

The greatest honor for these young people is to be accepted as members of an exclusive non-Jewish fraternity, a professional non-Jewish organization, athletic or social club. This is for them a symbol of their acceptance by the non-Jewish world, and that their Jewishness does not stand in their way.

As for marrying a non-Jewish girl or boy, this is vested with a particular dignity. An investigation carried on by a Hillel director among Jewish students in Northwestern University revealed that 25% who were asked if they would marry a non-Jew answered yes. Here it is not a question of people who have already fallen in love. These are students who speak in advance. The same 25% indicated that they had no particular association with Jews or Judaism.

Most of our Jewish youth speak neither Yiddish nor Hebrew, neither feel their Jewishness nor think in terms of it. Having been raised in other languages and cultures they belittle the treasures of our Jewish literature. The little Jewish nourishment they have is a translated Judaism, an *ersatz;* and this is why, until now, there has not been a single great American-born Jewish thinker of national outlook.

We come across people who aspire to leadership and influence in Jewish public life without Jewish spiritual aspirations. "Mediocrity occupies the highest places in leadership, the intellect has lost its place of respect in the leadership of the American Jewish community." This is a recent statement of Philip Klutznick, president of International B'nai Brith. There are leaders who do not know the letters of the Hebrew alphabet and some who once knew, but now have difficulty distinguishing between a *beth* and a *koph,* a *daleth* and a *resh,* a *gimel* and a *nun.*

At conferences of the Jewish community one sees a new type of younger leader who is a devoted worker for Israel and local Jewish institutions. But he lacks one thing— religious devotion. Mostly such leaders come to conferences not because of Jewish consciousness but to symbolize the link of their local community with the national organization. They are proud to be Jews and would not let a word be said to injure Jewish honor. Ask them, however, why they are proud of being Jews, and most will give a banal answer, picked up in the men's club, the sisterhood, the "Y", a sermon, or from a speech at a Brotherhood Week banquet. The phrase, "I'm proud to be a Jew," is the sum total of their spiritual equipment. Their knowledge extends only to fundraising. Where is the thread that binds this new type of Jewish communal volunteer to Judaism? Some day fundraising at its present pace is bound to come to an end. What will be the Jewish tie then?

The rise of the State of Israel no doubt stirred enthusiasm and strengthened Jewish consciousness in the younger generation. Gradually, however, the enthusiasm has cooled off. Many intellectuals in fact take the view that since the Jewish state exists, the security of the Jewish people in Israel is assured, hence there is no further need to maintain a separate Jewish community or traditional Jewish life in the diaspora.

"How great is the difference between my brother and my non-Jewish boy friend?", a Jewish girl argued with me. "Show me how my brother's Jewishness sets him apart from my boy friend. Both are non-religious. Their interests and habits are the same. My brother's home is not different from that of my future in-laws. Most Jewish young people I know behave like my brother and like my non-Jewish boy friend. Why all the commotion about my marrying a non-Jew? If I should take a Jewish husband, how would he differ from a non-Jewish one? My home will be no different. You say that the children will be split personalities, that they will be neither Jews nor Christians. What are my brother's children? In what sense are they Jews other than being born of Jewish parents? If my children won't be Jews, at least they will be Christians."

This is a major factor leading to mixed marriages. Among many of our Jewish youth it is not at all considered "mixed." They do not distinguish between Jewish and non-Jewish youth. Even those who did attend a *cheder* or a *shul* or a *Talmud Torah* were not afforded sufficient insulation against the non-Jewish influence around them.

Most of our Jewish youth are not interested in Jewish problems. Raised and brought up in Jewish homes, they nevertheless know nothing of religion and national character.

One cannot even carry on a conversation with most of them. There is no sign in their behavior and manners that they are children of a people constantly struggling for its security and future.

We do not know to what extent Sholem Asch was successful, through his "Christian" novels, in bringing Jewry and Christendom closer. We do know, however, that his *East River*, which is a paean in praise of intermarriage, has created a state of confusion in the minds of many young Jews. In discussing mixed marriages with them, I frequently hear references to Asch's books and his glorification of marriage between Jew and Christian.

In a study published in the *Catholic Digest*, dealing with the attitude of the general population to religious matters, it was shown that 75% of Protestants and 72% of Catholics were unwilling to have a member of their family marry a Jew. Of the Jews canvassed, 26% expressed themselves favorably on mixed marriages with Protestants and 24% with Catholics.

We are familiar with a case in which a Jewish youth married the daughter of devout Catholic parents. This tragedy broke his parents' heart and they died soon after. Unhappy in his marriage and suffering from pangs of conscience and guilt after his parents' death, the son fell sick. Feeling that his days were numbered, he sent for the rabbi and asked him to see that he receive a Jewish burial. His wife, who had frequently upbraided him for his Jewishness, would not agree that her husband and the father of her child be buried in a Jewish cemetery. When the rabbi appeared to fulfill this last wish, he was met with her answer—the priest she had brought to the hospital. The latter told the rabbi that at the time of marriage the husband had adopted Catholicism, to which he belonged not only during, but after, life.

With bitter irony the dying young man told the rabbi,

"I lost my Jewish soul to the Church and now they are claiming my body. Tell it to those who have been deceived; perhaps they will learn."

From the beginning of our dispersion we have known that in order to live as a minority and yet maintain our Jewish way of life and faith in our heritage, we must possess extraordinary persistence and sacrifice. This faith gave us strength and will to suffer and to struggle, and shielded us against assimilation. The Jew saw in the Torah the incorporation of all that is sacred and exalted. We regarded our prophets and sages as emissaries who brought us the heavenly word of God about happiness and justice for mankind.

There has been a change. We no longer appreciate Jewish teaching, culture, and ideals. The prestige of Jewish scholarship has fallen. Even religiously minded parents are happier when their children achieve success in their secular studies than in Jewish learning. This inferiority complex has even penetrated our rabbis. They take more pride in their non-Jewish academic training and their college degrees than in their Hebraic studies.

How can such rabbis strengthen Jewish consciousness in our youth when they glory most in their non-Jewish attainments and quote mainly from Christian scholars, instead of from the Torah, Prophets, and Midrashim?

How can they expect our youth to appreciate the Jewish heritage and be interested in Jewish literature when the rabbis themselves show no proper attitude to the Yiddish or Hebrew language, to Jewish culture, to the Hebrew book?

We stand face to face with the greatest danger in our history—our youth, the source of Jewish strength, is drying up. What force can prevent intermarriage and total assimilation if all that pertains to our non-Jewish neighbors, their behavior, their culture, is pictured to our youth as finer, more tasteful, and richer than our own?

At the 23rd Zionist Congress in Jerusalem, Dr. Nahum Goldmann, president of the World Zionist Organization, warned against exaggerated optimism and the feeling that our future as a nation is secure now that there is a Jewish state. A mood of indifference to the spiritual condition of Jewry has overcome a great portion of our people.

We all grew up in the fight against assimilation. The German type was child's play in comparison with the American. The assimilated American Jew has no ideology and needs none. He lives well. He is not even aware anything is lacking. The hardest thing to fight is a vacuum.

Tens of thousands of Jews have become assimilated without benefit of any theory or philosophy—they were merely brought up that way. In a poll among Jewish students the question was asked what makes them Jews. The majority answered, "Because our parents are Jews."

The danger of widespread ignorance, assimilation, and mixed marriages among Jewish youth is increasing because of the apathy in Jewish circles. Recently because of increased membership in synagogues and temples, optimists have seen the return of our Jewish youth. This optimism is not only illusory but actually dangerous. It has the effect of freeing us from responsibility through declaring, "There have been times like this before; and Israel will not falter; the situation cannot be so bad as the alarmists picture it."

"Let us look the bitter truth right in the face," said Dr. Goldmann recently. Jewish survival is now undergoing the greatest danger in the history of the Jewish people. Six million were physically annihilated by the Nazis. More than two and a half million behind the Iron Curtain are spiritually cut off from us. The danger exists that many Jewish communities will become spiritually decimated because of assimilation and mixed marriages.

In Prof. Eli Ginzberg's "Agenda for American Jews" the author points to the growing ignorance and the rising minimization of Jewish spiritual values which are the greatest dangers threatening the Jewish community. There are Jewish organizations functioning, which, if they have any connection at all, are not linked by the bonds of a common Jewish continuity and philosophy, nor through moral influence of a higher spiritual motivation, and are allied only by the threads of a common fund-raising campaign.

The leaders of these campaigns are certainly serious men devoted to their work. They are not, however, possessed of an oversupply of Jewish knowledge and cannot distinguish among the various beneficiaries for which the campaigns are conducted.

We have become first rate campaigners. Our organizational technique has reached the level of an exact science. But as for doing anything for Jewish youth, everything is conducted in a very doubtful fashion. Every activity emphasizes the entertainment and recreational, rather than the idealistic and spiritual, purposes behind the efforts of the organizers.

Most programs and activities of Jewish youth organizations consist of sport and entertainment, imposing few responsibilities upon the members. This is the greatest error of the leaders, thinking that in this way they will succeed in attaching the youth to Jewish life. On the contrary, if we want to tie our young people to an ideal, to a way of life, we can do so only by calling them to stern responsibility and discipline. We must stop talking about Jewish continuity, about the Jewish future, in an abstract way, as though we were dealing not with time but with eternity itself.

Through our eyes we see a generation passing, but we see only pale symptoms of a generation rising. Between the passing and the coming Jewish generations there exists a difference not only in depth and quantity of Jewishness, but in basic content.

In order to insure survival we must devote all our strength, all our energy, all our attention and anxiety, to the problem of Jewish youth. Other problems are petty and of little consequence. This is not the property of any particular faction or element but of the entire Jewish community. All Jewish life depends on Jewish youth, the heirs who will take over and carry on our heritage, our obligations, our peculiar national religion and way of life.

"Bury me not in the land of Egypt," Jacob bade his sons. With a look into the far future, our patriarch meant that Jews who have lived among the nations of the world should maintain their traditions, not to assimilate and lose themselves in the majority, but to call themselves Israel again in the name of their forefathers.

To prevent the spread of ignorance, assimilation, and mixed marriage among Jewish youth, we must teach them to understand the beauty, the ethics, and the greatness of Jewish values, the ideas and ideals which nourished and maintained their people in all generations and in all times, the strength to rise in revolt in the ghettos, and the heroism to build and defend the land of Israel.

We must teach our youth that to be a Jew is to swim against the stream, that Jewishness exacts a price and it is worth that price. This was the way of our parents, and herein lies the strength of our survival. Only then will they feel what it is to live with the ideal of Jewishness, and like their parents, will they take pleasure in paying the price of difference—the price of being a Jew.

CHAPTER VII

THE JEWISH DAUGHTER AND
MIXED MARRIAGES

Among no other people or religion does the woman occupy so prominent a place, or is she so idealized and respected as among the Jews. The Torah, in recounting the life and influence of the patriarch Abraham, tells of his wife Sarah, who, like her husband, shared in and contributed to the birth of Judaism. We are told that Abraham had a high respect for his wife's opinion. "And Abraham hearkened unto the voice of Sarah" (Genesis 16:12) and again in Genesis 21:12: "In all that Sarah hath said unto thee hearken unto her." Our sages interpreted this as meaning, "If the wife is short, bend down and listen to her advice" (Baba Metzia 59a). The wives of the patriarchs—Sarah, Rebecca, Rachel, and Leah—are accounted as mothers and builders of the house of Israel. "May the Lord make the woman that is come into thy house like Rachel and like Leah, which two did build the house of Israel" (Ruth 4:11). Before God gave the Torah to the people of Israel, He first bade Moses talk to the women: "Thou shalt thus say to the House of Jacob" (Exodus 19:3). A talmudic comment on this passage reads:

> " 'To the house of Jacob'—this means the women. 'The children of Israel'—this means the men. God said, 'If I do not call the women first they will abolish the Torah.' Therefore it is written, 'Thus shalt thou say to the House of Jacob.' "
>
> Shemot Rabbah

The ethical and social laws of Judaism place the woman on a pedestal. A child's religious identity is accounted

69

through his mother; it is the line of the mother that determines the child's Jewishness. The happiness of a family is dependent on the husband's attitude of respect toward the wife: "Let a man ever be careful to honor his wife, because God's blessing is found in a man's house only for the sake of his wife" (Baba Metzia 59a); and further: "Any Jew that has no wife lives without joy, without blessing, without happiness. Rabbi Bar Ula adds, 'Without peace'" (Jebamot 62b).

Two books of the Scriptures bear the names of women, Ruth and Esther. Jewish women were included among the prophets. Deborah the prophetess is honored as a mother in Israel. Throughout the history of the Jewish people the woman always played a foremost role—a heroic one, in fact. She took an active part and had a vital role in the preservation and existence of her people.

We mention all this to expose the inaccuracy of those who say that the Jewish religion looks upon the female as inferior. The Torah, the Scriptures, and the Prophets, the Talmud and the Midrash, attributed vital importance to the wife in maintenance of Jewish traditions such as no other people or civilization has granted its women. Judaism has crowned the woman with its noblest title, "mistress of the home." The Jewish mother *is* the home. Rabbi Jose said, "I have never called my wife 'my wife' but I call her 'my home'" (Shabbat 118b).

The Jewish community from the beginning realized that the Jewish daughter is the foundation of the Jewish home and the keystone of Jewish national survival. Our sages say that in the exodus from Egypt it was "in the merit of our wives and virtuous women that our forefathers were delivered from Egypt" (Sotah). In our own day the Jewish daughter with her faith, courage, initiative, and devotion has been a factor of great inspiration in upbuilding and strengthening the new State of Israel. Every day the Jewish woman makes her contribution to the support of Jewish folk life and national survival.

One of the finest qualities of the Jewish woman—a quality which drew great praise from our sages and was a source of pride to our people for centuries—was her modesty. She was renowned for her modest God-fearing behavior, her loyalty and devotion to her husband and children, her patience, courage, and inspiration in holding the family together.

The modern age has opened wide the doors of the Jewish home and has made great changes in Jewish family life and in the character, thinking, and conduct of the Jewish daughter. The old, intimate Jewish atmosphere is no more. The close warmth which became part of the being of the members of the family and which held them securely to each other has either vanished or is greatly attenuated. The Jewish home has become devoid of practical Jewishness. The intimacy, the devotion, the love and concern of one for another—all these are gone. It is nothing more than a convenient place where one takes one's meals and sleeps.

Children grow to maturity amid the psychic experience of a rather impersonal family life. They are not familiar with that sense of family responsibility which intimacy and love create. The nervous drive that children absorb at home develops within them the impulse to grow out of their home, to become independent, and start their own frantic chase for the things of this world. This striving is developed much earlier among girls than among boys. Why this is so is not within my competence to explain. The fact is that Jewish girls are on the whole more grasping, more self-centered, and domineering at home than are their brothers.

There is a widespread view that daughters are generally more attached to their parents than sons. When a daughter marries it is supposed that she visits her parents' home more often and shows a greater interest in them than her brothers do. No formal research on the differences in filial attitude between brother and sister has yet been carried out and as a result no rules can be drawn on the subject. Our own observation has been that in those Jewish homes where there is no great discrepancy in cultural level between the parents and children, and where there is no mutual disparagement between parents, the children are raised in respect, and son and daughter alike are loyally attached to their parents. In those homes, on the other hand, where children acquire an academic education and look down upon their parents, there is estrangement between the generations irrespective of the sex of the children.

It is a fact that because girls are more sensitive as little children and parents bestow more attention on them and are more lenient with them, many Jewish daughters grow up spoiled and arrogant without respect or appreciation for their elders. When they later become independent and take up a career they dominate life at home and have little regard for their parents' feelings.

One of the cardinal reasons that mixed marriages most often occur between Jewish youths and gentile girls is this over-tender upbringing of Jewish girls, in which parents often extend themselves beyond their financial ability to give them every advantage and indulgence. When they grow up and are ready for marriage they seek a husband as complaisant and indulgent as their parents were. Their behavior is that of a child-aristocrat. Their greatest ideal is fine clothes, expensive jewelry, and an elaborately furnished home, and they do not hesitate to let this be known to the young men who court them. Many are frightened off by the sheer unreality (as far as they are concerned) of this fantasy of many Jewish girls. They fear they cannot cope with the demands of that kind of life. This has the effect of driving them into non-Jewish circles. Here they find friendships among non-Jewish girls who may appreciate the personal character of the Jewish boy rather than his ability to provide them with a life of luxury.

A Jewish young man, who was intermarried for a few years and later divorced, complained to us bitterly, blaming Jewish girls for his own unhappy marriage experience.

"I am a good tradesman," he said. "I earn a decent income.

When I took out a Jewish girl she would ask to be brought only to the most expensive places. She would talk of a wealthy home, costly furs, and a luxurious life. Her mother constantly mentioned that she hoped her daughter would have a better lot in life than she had had. They scared me off. I felt that with my earnings I could make a comfortable and decent home for a wife; but not the kind the mother and daughter had pictured. Most Jewish girls whom I took out were more interested in my income than in my person.

"I became acquainted with a gentile girl whose outlook was more modest and limited. She did not ask for too much and did not look for a life of ease and luxury. She was more interested in me than in my money, and struck me as making a better wife than any of the Jewish girls I knew. When we fell in love I saw no obstacle whatsoever to our union. At first I really felt happy. As it happened, later we decided through our experiences that people of different religions were people of different worlds; that when one is raised in a certain religion, even though one may be no believer, nonetheless the cultural implications and the way of life of the religion are deeply ingrained—and we decided to part. This is something we did not think of or anticipate at the time of the wedding. But the fault for my unhappy and broken married life is that of the Jewish girls and their exaggerated demands on life. They do not want to understand that most Jewish young men who seek marriage want friendship and a faithful partner who will know how to manage a modest household and be able to establish a sound foundation for a happy future."

We cannot generalize that this applies to all Jewish girls, but it remains true in large measure that many Jewish young women are attracted by outward appearance, dazzled by luxurious dress and pleasures, extravagant in their behavior, and expect far too much personal and material satisfaction from marriage. There is no longer the traditional Jewish modesty, the pious decency, the readiness to dedicate oneself to the future of the family as a "mother in Israel."

What has helped bring this about is the tendency, attributable to various factors, to single sons out for a traditional religious training; daughters need no such education. This is an utterly false concept. Jewish education is as essential for the daughter as for the son. The daughter is the backbone of the family. She personifies the home, and upon her depends the practice of Jewishness, celebration of the festivals, creation of a Jewish atmosphere, maintenance of the home, and raising children in the Jewish way of life.

But many Jewish parents do not think this way. They provide their daughters with lessons in music, singing, elocution, dancing, but there is no time for Jewish training. As a result they grow up with a feeling of disparagement towards their parents and a tenuous bond with their origins. Most Jewish girls lack a sense of rootedness in Jewish life. The threads are quite fragile and they have no feeling of fear about cutting them.

A father complains, "My daughter is a beauty, educated and cultivated. A young college professor is in love with her. The marriage is taking place in the Presbyterian church. How can I attend a wedding where all can see my daughter being married by a Christian clergyman?"

"Doesn't she take or seek any guidance from her parents?"

"She's old enough to know her own mind—it's her life. 'All people are alike; all religions are the same,' is what she answers us."

This is the price parents pay for minimizing their daughters' Jewish education. It is vital for the future of the Jewish family and Jewish life for the daughter to learn that the Jewish virtues of modesty and family purity are of greater value than diamonds and clothes; they will then not find it necessary to seek peace for their nerves with psychiatrists and psychologists.

Our sages tell us that in the time of the Temple the fifteenth day of the month of Ab was one of the merriest of the calendar. On that day the maidens went out to draw the attention of the youths to their charms, their wisdom, their family piety, and other virtues. On that day all had one thing in common: they were dressed in borrowed white clothes in order not to embarrass the poorer ones who could not clothe themselves as richly (Taanot 26b).

The Jewish maiden was permitted to boast of all her qualities save one—external ornament and dress. This was considered superficial show which reflected vain pride rather than qualities of character and good breeding.

Personal qualities, a plain and modest attitude, moral behavior and piety—these were the highest qualifications of the Jewish woman, on which the Jewish people prided itself through long generations. She was thus described thousands of years ago by Solomon, wisest of men:

> "Grace is deceitful and beauty is vain;
> But a woman who feareth the Lord, she shall be praised!
> Give her of the fruit of her hands;
> And let her works praise her in the gates."
>
> Proverbs 31:30

CHAPTER VIII

MIXED MARRIAGES IN SMALL COMMUNITIES

Thousands of Jewish families dispersed in small communities in the United States and Canada are in danger of being submerged among the general population due to the corrosive environment of provincial life—an environment which leads to intermarriage and which may eventually leave no trace of them. Hundreds of Jewish families who were among pioneers in the development of trade, creators of Main Streets in provincial towns in America, have already been completely lost, and their descendants are active members of Christian denominations.

Unfortunately very little attention is given this problem by Jewish communal workers and by the Jewish public in general. The apathy of the East European city Jew toward the country Jew—the *yishuvnik*—has apparently been transferred to this continent. The Jew in the small town is left to himself and his own resources.

Although the literal translation of "country Jew" corresponds to the old *yishuvnik*, there is actually a great difference between the two. While in the old country the *yishuvnik* was generally a Jew who dwelt in a village, one among hundreds of ignorant, backward peasants, a simple unlettered fellow—the provincial Jew of our continent lives in a sizable town which is just as modern as the big city, except that the Jewish community is a small one; its life and character and environment are quite different from that of East Europe.

The *yishuvnik*, or "Jew of the Dorf," had problems stemming from his separation from the larger Jewish community,

76

but his family's future was secure because of the great chasm between Jew and gentile. However, in the smaller communities where Jew and non-Jew are equal citizens and where religion is separate from the state, a type of assimilation arises which threatens to submerge the Jew completely.

It is a Jewish trend to be urban dwellers. The only motive which impelled pioneers in days gone by (and today) to settle in small places was the possibility of making a livelihood. So long as a Jew makes a living in a city with a large and concentrated Jewish community, even a modest living, he will not settle in the country. If he does so, it is solely for economic reasons.

At the beginning, when he is up to his neck in business, he has room for no other considerations. When he succeeds more or less in stabilizing his affairs he has some leisure to look around at his environment and his home, and his growing family. He suddenly comes upon problems about which he has never dreamed, and he finds that they give him far more trouble than business problems.

In many of the towns where there is a large organized community, a synagogue, a temple, a center, a Talmud Torah, a Sunday school, Jewish life goes on and he does not feel cut off and remote. His family problem only becomes urgent when the children grow up and are ready for marriage. It is worse for the Jews in the small spots—and there are many of them—which contain only a few Jewish families. There is no Jewish school and no Jewish life. The home is empty of Jewishness.

When the non-Jewish holidays arrive, all the stores are shut, a holiday atmosphere prevails which infiltrates the Jewish home. Jewish children grow to see no difference between the customs of their parents and those of their non-Jewish neighbors. Why then should they not fall in love, and marry one or another of their non-Jewish friends?

In general the life of the small town Jew is completely different from that of the Jew in the larger cities. Where there is an intense and active Jewish life, there are synagogues, organizations, Y.M.H.A.'s, ideological movements, entertainments, Jewish institutions for all—men, women, and children. If anyone wishes to grow and develop within a Jewish framework, there is ample opportunity. Those in the large cities who isolate themselves fall away from the Jewish community like amputated limbs. They seek non-Jewish society, and there they also seek their future mates. They do it not unwillingly, and not because they have no alternate choice. In these cases, neither the Jewish environment nor the Jewish community is at fault. These self-hating Jewish sons and daughters suffer from inferiority complexes. This is the obsequious desire to find favor in other people's eyes. There was a deep-rooted complex in our parents, and grandparents from Europe—to flatter, to fawn and genuflect, before the non-Jew. Their actions cannot be blamed on Jewish society or Jewish institutions. Had they wished to swim in the stream of Jewish life they had all the opportunities, for Jewish communal life in the large city possesses a social climate from which everyone can choose.

For the "country" Jew the atmosphere, the cultural opportunities, of the metropolis are lacking. Jew and non-Jew meet more intimately, in business establishments, Rotary and Kiwanis clubs, Y.M.C.A.'s. They associate as neighbors, and their women and children mingle freely. They attend social gatherings and sport events together, visit one another's homes, and develop a bond of intimacy.

It is difficult then to lead a traditional Jewish life. Unwittingly, the Jew is absorbed into the community. He may struggle not to be engulfed and severed. But such a one is only a speck in a vast sea. He and his family are also drawn into the waters, and his children intermarry.

Much worse off is the plight of the Jew in a small town with no more than ten or twenty Jewish families. Such communities are strewn over the American continent. The Jew here is even more intimate and friendly with his non-Jewish neighbor. He may want to spend an evening amid Jewish surroundings, but this is denied the Jew living among a handful of Jewish families.

The monthly B'nai Brith meetings and collections for various Jewish funds are not greeted with enthusiasm. Often these activities are frowned on or condemned. The only things heard at Jewish meetings are anti-defamation and other Jewish problems. Having lived intimately with non-Jews the local Jews do not feel the need for anti-defamation action. Without contact with Jewish life they do not sense the afflictions of Jews abroad. When they give money for Jewish causes it is because they feel that thus they may settle their Jewish obligations.

These small town Jews are more than glad to take part in the activities of the community. Through compulsive need to demonstrate their devotion to local affairs, they work hard and are elected to office.

The church plays a large role in the life of the country dweller. Most Christian inhabitants of the smaller communities are religious, conservative-minded church-goers. Nearly everyone goes on Sunday, and many belong to Bible study classes. Religion, in fact, is the only element which at times divides the country Jew and his non-Jewish neighbor. Notwithstanding the fact that most Christians have respect for the people who gave them a God in the Old Testament, they feel nevertheless that there exists a division, when one goes to church on Sundays and the other does not. This is the only factor preventing complete fusion. *They* are Jews and *we* are Christians.

Quite often Christians say to their Jewish friends, "Look, we work together in all community affairs and belong to the same clubs; our children work and play together; our wives share in the yearly church bazaar; why not become members in our church?"

Many are thus influenced. Though most are members in name only and do not participate in church services, we know of cases in several small communities where Jews have become board members of the church. But most of the children regularly attend the Sunday school.

Thus bit by bit the barrier is broken down. Families live intimately, children grow up together. When the Jewish child introduces his parents for the first time to a non-Jewish beloved, utter confusion breaks out. The parents do not approve, though under the circumstances it was to be expected. A deep-rooted distaste for mixed marriages, stemming from Father Abraham, opposes this union. The parents become aware that their antagonism will not prevail. A rift arises. The children become bitter, look on their parents as enemies, sometimes fling in their faces some offensive anti-Semitic epithet they think applicable to their parents, not themselves.

We know of instances where parents have sacrificed themselves to provide the finest and the best for their children, who, reared in a non-Jewish environment, nevertheless look down upon them. That iota of observance at Passover and the high holidays is regarded as an anachronism.

The younger Jewish generation in North America is not in harmony with the older. In large Jewish communities the behavior patterns of the children differ greatly, but the conflict is even more clearly visible in the lives of the provincial Jews.

In general, youth will not be bound to a life of monotony and boredom. No matter where the young man finds himself, even in the most isolated and remote places, he will discover ways of passing his time, and socially expressing his youthful emotions. If there is a dance or other youthful entertainment in the town, the Jewish younger folk are the first to obtain tickets. Quite often they are organizers, and with some skill in sport become very popular. The press gives them the appropriate publicity, though no mention of their Jewishness is made. Their parents are very proud. The Jewish young man soon learns to appreciate his importance, and no longer looks to his parents for advice. He ignores or disdains Jewish parties, where young Jews feel and participate as strangers. On Jewish festivals the experience becomes an ordeal. There is nothing that interests them, not the rabbi's English sermon, nor the translations of the prayers. Jewishness is something that has remained for the "old folks."

They have been very frank in admitting to us this feeling of greater comfort in a non-Jewish group. Under these circumstances, the parents should not be surprised that their children intermarry.

There are even Jewish children who believe that by intermarrying they are only practising what many large Jewish organizations propagandize through their "Public Relations," "Interfaith," "Brotherhood," or "Goodwill" councils.

A Jewish boy and his non-Jewish fiancée came to our house, and he railed against his parents, who were alarmed and hysterical about his planned marriage. He talked about them in tones of annoyance and impatience. They were born here, he told us, Americanized. Surely one would think they would take a "modern outlook." Though members of the temple, they still nurtured the "old country" traditions. He was a faithful son, loved his father and mother, so he was willing to sacrifice his modern ideals and have a Jewish *chuppah,* after which he would be officially married in the Presbyterian church, where his future in-laws were prominent members.

When we told this young man that under no conditions would we officiate at his marriage, he looked aghast and bewildered. "Rabbi, I am amazed at you! Why, you are a member of the public relations committee in town! How can you be unwilling to perform an act of goodwill between Jew and non-Jew? Can there be a better gesture of intimacy and brotherhood than intermarriage?"

We interpreted our view of public relations, explained that the parents of his fiancée were as much against this union as his own parents, that it was not an act of "goodwill" on his part. On the contrary, since most intermarriages end in tragedy, it only made for illfeeling and misunderstanding. Furthermore, there was no need to speak so disparagingly about his parents. The youth exclaimed with great venom, "It is clear to me now why Hitler exterminated the Jews. My parents and you, rabbi, with your fanatic, old country behavior, will make it so that a Hitler will arise in this country. . . ."

Estranged, untaught, unlettered, often anti-Semitic, are the grown Jewish boys and girls in small towns. Jewish history is a blank page to them. They have learnt nothing from recent experiences. The Jewish catastrophe in Europe has left them cold, and the massacre of six million Jews has in no wise affected them.

In provincial Jewry also there is a coolness of Jewish young men towards Jewish girls. One would rather date a non-Jewish girl than a gracious and beautiful Jewess. One can readily give many reasons, but the fact remains that where Jewish boys in small towns marry Jewesses, the girls come mainly from the larger cities. Thus the lot of the Jewish girl is more difficult than that of the boy. The parents feel the loneliness that descends upon their daughters. Should one refuse to enter into the wider non-Jewish social functions of the community, there is nothing left but to sit alone at home. Therefore parents with relatives in larger communities send their daughters there, either to college or to work, with the hope that they find suitable Jewish mates. A monthly allowance is arranged. Nevertheless, this does not rule out the possibility that a Jewish girl will fall in love with a non-Jew. However, it is in the main the Jewish boys who create the problem of intermarriage.

The problem is fraught with danger on other grounds, because in many intermarriages the young people are absorbed in the Jewish community and are treated as equals. The Jew can still not avoid feeling that by marrying outside the fold, he has committed an injustice against parents, the Jewish community, and all Jewry. He may seek to rectify this wrong by becoming one of the most active members in the community. We know of several towns wherein the president of the Community Council, the chairman of the Welfare Fund, the president of B'nai B'rith Lodge, all have non-Jewish wives. Often these wives are active in Hadassah, and the sisterhood of the Welfare Fund. The Jewish parents who at first were antagonistic are now very proud of their non-Jewish daughter-in-law. They are seated at the head table at every important meeting. The Jewish youth is not blind; he sees and knows all. When a Jewish boy falls in love with a non-Jewess, the parents beseech the rabbi to speak to their son, to convince him not to take this step that will bring disaster and grief upon them. The first thing the lad does, of course, is point to the president of the congregation, the president of B'nai B'rith, the president of the Jewish Community Council, all of whom have non-Jewish wives, all active and respected in the community.

Such conduct of a Jewish community is one of the greatest factors in abetting the spread of intermarriage. It constitutes a silent sanction by the community. It weakens the determination and will of parents, as well as that of the rabbi.

We have had dozens of such cases. Couples have thrown back at parents and rabbi the precedent set by the man holding one of the highest posts in the Jewish community whose wife is Christian. The official bulletin prints news of mixed weddings. Jewish women's organizations are friendly and hospitable to the wives. Opposition to mixed marriages thereby comes to be nothing more than a worn anachronism —a vestigial remnant of the backward ghetto life of the old country.

"Rabbi, you are a modern person," argued most of the young people; "forget the Jewish world of the old days. We live in a modern era. What is past is past. Everyone is equal now. The old difference between Christian and Jew is gone. Why, the president of the Jewish community has a Christian wife, and my mother tells me she is much better than a Jewish wife." This exaggerated friendliness to members of mixed marriages, the distribution of highest honors to them, and the esteem Jewish mothers accord the conduct of Christian wives, lowers the dignity of Jewish daughters in the eyes of the sons. There are over five million Jews in America. How many can be included in the final accounting of Jewish survival? How many have already left us spiritually and can be dropped from this count? How many have vanished without trace into the environment? How many have led their children to marriage in the church? How many are members of churches?

We have no exact statistics of these "lost tribes," but we know that they do exist; they are forever lost to the community of Israel.

Once we were on a visit to a large Jewish provincial community. The Jewish retailer mentioned rather casually that every year at Passover dozens of non-Jews came into his store from a nearby small town to buy matzos. This curious fact intrigued us. It reminded us of something similar among the Christian great-grandchildren of the Spanish Marranos, who to this very day, on the eve of Passover, carry on the clandestine practice of going to market to buy horseradish (the "bitter herb" of the Haggadah). We took the trip to the nearby small town and it did not take us long to learn that the chief of police was one of the matzah buyers. After a lengthy conversation with prominent families we noticed that if letters were eliminated from either the beginning or the end of the various "Irish" names, they would emerge as Jewish. Several Christian families confessed to us that they bought matzos every year a few days before Easter, which falls close to Passover. Why did they do this? They did not know. It had been the practice of their parents, which they had taken over.

Somewhat later in my enquiries several Christian families admitted knowing they were of Jewish descent. Some recalled their great-grandparents who occasionally used a Yiddish word. One prominent citizen insisted that we visit his home and meet his family.

We accepted. He introduced us to his family, his wife, and three handsome children. His home was well furnished. While I was chatting with the wife and children the father excused himself and left the room. Ten minutes later he returned with a photograph. It was of a young boy wearing a *yarmulka*, wrapped in a small *tallis*, and holding a *siddur*.

"This is my father," said the Christian *paterfamilias*, with great respect. "It was taken at his bar mitzvah," he added, wiping the perspiration from his brow. "Now you understand why I was so insistent that you visit my family. I wanted to show you the photograph and I also wanted my family to become acquainted with a rabbi."

"Do your wife and children know you are of Jewish descent?"

"Of course they do. When we got married my parents were still alive. My father was Jewish. My mother was Irish. My children know that grandpa was Jewish. The Lord Jesus Christ was also a Jew," he said aloud, for the children to hear. He told us that the largest department store in the town had been founded by a Jew. From his small general store there had developed the large store now administered by his grandchildren.

"Do his grandchildren know that they have Jewish ancestry?"

"Of course. They still remember their old Jewish grandfather and their Christian grandmother. When we meet we talk openly about our ancestry."

We spent a whole day at this town and left with a picture of a whole Jewish community erased from history and from the community of Israel. Today a few Jewish families live there, thoroughly assimilated. Their fate will no doubt be the same, and they will be lost to the Jewish collective.

In a city with a population of more than 100,000 we met the mayor of many years. He too was of Jewish origin. His mother was a Jewess from Vienna, who still lived with him. His father was a Christian. Sometimes his mother made *gefilte fish* and *kneidlach*. At Passover he ate matzos. His wife and children were active members of the Presbyterian church.

We could tell of hundreds of such cases, about Jewish peddlers from Poland, Galicia, Ukraine, Russia, and Romania—pioneers in small and large communities, first storekeepers on Main Street, who left behind esteemed Jewish families which in the course of years have been completely lost.

The state of affairs is not improving. Will we continue to remain indifferent to the epidemic? Certainly an attitude of optimism, ignoring the dangerous situation, is easier and more restful than one which faces the facts directly. The facts are that if the first Jewish residents, who in the main came with Central Europe's ingrained religious and national traditions —people who brought Jewish life from Europe—if these were incapable of withstanding assimilationist pressure, and their families have disappeared through mixed marriages, what are the prospects several generations later with Jewish inhabitants who are of the second or third generation?

If one looks with open eyes at Jewish small town life, one can see a few elderly Jews conducting a Sabbath minyan in the synagogue or temple. Most Canadian-born Jews in the provinces do not attend synagogue. The late Friday night services and the attractions of the rabbi's sermons, the social hour, community singing—these are feebly attended. Often no more than the quorum of ten comes to the services. The recital of kaddish, the yahrzeit, and Yizkor make up Jewish religious life.

The Jewish population in most of the provincial towns is decentralized—dispersed among the general population. Jewish children cannot meet with each other or play together as often as in a large Jewish settlement. Jewish parents have little opportunity to come in contact with masses of Jews except for those who are perennial delegates to Jewish conferences. There is nothing to inspire them to strengthen or continue Jewish life. Their home is emptied of the spirit of

Israel and of the sense of belonging. Most Jews in the towns have received very little Jewish education, and are highly vulnerable. One need not be an alarmist to fear that Jewish social and communal life in the provinces will be assimilated and that ultimately thousands of Jewish families will be lost to the community of Israel.

The poison of assimilation, the conscious or unconscious alienation from group life, is particularly felt in Jewish education. A large number of Jewish children get no Jewish education at all, particularly in the smaller towns which cannot maintain a rabbi. A generation is growing up "which does not know Joseph," or anything of the Jewish past, Jewish heroism or Jewish martyrdom. Jewish speech is no longer heard, except perhaps from a grandfather or grandmother. The majority of parents who send their children for a few hours a week to the Talmud Torah do not do so because of conscience or understanding, but through external pressure or the influence of the rabbi.

The position of the rabbi in the towns is a chapter in itself. Generally he is engaged not for the community's own purposes as its spiritual leader, but to "show off" to the non-Jewish community, to represent them at non-Jewish clubs and to deputize for the Jewish community at all public undertakings.

In a survey on Jewish life in small towns by Dr. Max Baer, national director of the B'nai B'rith Vocational Bureau, who had inquired about everything and everybody in Jewish life in the provinces, there was not a word about the percentage of mixed marriages. He wrote that in certain towns on a question about Jewish education, the answer was "People here feel that is our biggest need for our children." This is the position of the rabbi as to Jewish education. Even those who send their children to a Jewish school do so only for the sake of appearances. Either the parents or the child want a big bar mitzvah party. This is, of course, a chapter in itself.

Most parents, satisfied with a bit of Judaism, send their children to a Sunday school. In general this "Bible story Jewishness" is disastrous for Jewish education, because for various

reasons it has been altered into a kindergarten of utter ignorance and chaos. The Sunday school in small towns is twice
as bad, since the teaspoonful of superficial Jewish education
is generally served by young men and women who are complete ignoramuses on the subject.

Jewish life there is completely of a social character, grouped
around B'nai B'rith activities, dinners, parties, dances, sports
activities. To belong to B'nai B'rith is as obligatory as to belong to a synagogue was for a Jew in Eastern Europe. Hillel
Foundation, anti-defamation work, the modicum of philanthropy that the B'nai B'rith lodge undertakes—all create the
feeling that this fulfills the sum of duties and obligations a
Jew owes to his community.

The annual campaigns of the United Jewish Appeal for
local and overseas funds creates some kind of Jewish awakening. Meetings are convened, speakers come to address the
community and appeal for money. They touch on general
Jewish problems.

The Zionist movement has not struck deep roots in North
America. The directors of the Zionist Organization are quite
aware that the mailing list of the movement and its membership exists only on paper. In each town there used to be a
number of individuals of the older generation—*chovave-
Zion*—who represented the community at a Zionist conference and at national conventions. With the passing of the
older generation, the Zionist ideal has died out.

With establishment of the State of Israel the world feeling
of national pride also filled the hearts of provincial Jews.
Local newspapers devoted headlines to stories of Jewish heroism and the struggle against the Arabs. The majority of the
Christian population which, as we have said, is religious-
minded, congratulated their Jewish neighbors, the people
which gave the world the Bible, for having re-won the Holy
Land. The fact that Jews have become a nation among other
nations with a heroic fighting army, with their own machinery
of government, cabinet ministers, representation in the U.N.
—all this has made the hearts of Jews swell with pride.

Regrettably, however, this has been no more than a transient phenomenon. The sentiment towards the State of Israel in the larger Jewish communities has for a number of reasons become lukewarm. The pride and enthusiasm of provincial communities have cooled off. The fact that lately we have heard of communities declining to give larger contributions for Israel and the JDC on the excuse that the money is needed for local needs evidences a sloughing off of Jewish responsibilities. If their excuse were true, our leadership should be highly satisfied. International funds for overseas causes would have suffered, but in compensation Jewish life for the small dispersed communities would be all the more conscious and vital, and perhaps this eventually would have paid off.

The real picture, unfortunately, is not so. The reasons given are simply a result of growing apathy. The bond the small town Jew had with Israel through his annual payment to the United Jewish Appeal, which helped give him the feeling that he was linked up with Jewish fate, is disappearing.

These facts give us a rather tragic picture of the Jewish future. Now that the dykes against the stream of assimilation and spiritual decline have been pierced, this stream has become a raging torrent. There are scores of Jewish communities, small and large, in Canada and the U.S.A. where today there cannot be found a single Jewish family without a mixed marriage. Their children marry non-Jews and they follow the religious paths of the non-Jewish side. In a large provincial town I know of a grandfather who recites the *mussaf* portion of the Sabbath prayers and is Torah reader on the high holidays. His grandchildren are faithful members of the local Lutheran church.

A woman once came to us dressed in black with an old fashioned *siddur* in her hand, and asked us to tell her what it was. When we said this was a prayerbook "from the old country" she told us with tears that her father had died the previous day. Before his death he had asked to place in his

grave the "old country prayerbook." Since the father had
left several Hebrew books she wanted to know which of
them was the "old country prayerbook." She buried it with
her father in the Methodist churchyard.

A colleague once told me that on behalf of the Chautauqua
—an organization which sends rabbis to lecture to students
in universities—he happened to visit a famous university
in a provincial city. His lectures on Jewish religion, philosophy, and ethics made an impression on the professors and
student body.

When he met the students later he noticed that the dean
would nod and mention to him, "They stem from your faith."

When the rabbi inquired about this remark the dean
replied that the parents of the students were well-to-do
citizens of Jewish origin, large contributors to the university
and faithful church members, and he wanted them to feel
some pride in the great scholars and teachers of their people.
I am not concerned with whether the dean's purpose was
proper or not. Actually I was doubtful about this point, as
the students in question seemed quite unaware of their
Jewish descent. My friend was interested, however. On
inquiry he learned that the students were children of prominent well-born Christian families whose grandparents and
great-grandparents were Jews who had intermarried.

Has any national organization ever done anything concrete
about Jewish survival in the broad and dispersed American
Jewish continent? There is the wide chasm which separates
the Jewish areas of concentration and the smaller places.
The old belittling of the rural dweller is still deeply rooted
in the Jews of the larger cities. Leaders of the large communities do consider the provincial Jews as important—they
are summoned to conferences; they are asked for their share
of the national Jewish funds; their needs at the sessions are
listened to with patience. The tragedy, however, is that
nobody gives a thought or pays attention to their fate, to
the fate of their families or the future of their communities.

If a guest from a large community visits a provincial town to address a meeting or banquet which has been prepared for weeks ahead at great effort and expense, he sees only festive faces. What he does not see is the humdrum greyness of their daily life. The guest comes for a day, or overnight, and meets the cream of the local leadership, who are too embarrassed to tell the guest what the real situation is— to expose the full poverty of Jewish life.

Even now Jewish families are dropping from the common stem of Israel without leaving a trace. What can be done to rescue them from being swallowed up spiritually and physically by the Christian majority? What effective means can be used against the epidemic of mixed marriages? What is needed, first of all, is an awakening national responsibility for Jewish spiritual life in the smaller town. Religious and national bodies and organizations must place on their agenda the strengthening of Jewish life everywhere. There must be a wide and full apparatus with the participation of all religious and national Jewish organizations interested in Jewish survival, who must link themselves with the smallest Jewish community on a basis of equality, not on one of superciliousness. Even those communities with only two or three Jewish families must be included. Parents should be spoken to regularly about the danger of assimilation, to which the provincial Jew is particularly exposed. A constant campaign must be waged against mixed marriages.

This organization must become a popular movement, to recruit a type of *chalutz*-pioneer from among Jewish movements whose ideal should be to work and plow the neglected soil of Judaism.

We appreciate that we are quite a distance from that ideal pioneer period, particularly on this continent. Let these chalutzim be paid professionally, but not be like the periodic speech-makers who come for a day or two and leave immediately. They should remain for a considerable while in each Jewish settlement, get together with the rabbi, and devote their entire energy and time to working energetically with the Jewish inhabitants, helping them to resist the all-consuming environment.

Other denominations are doing this very thing. They send emissaries, visit the most remote communities. Among us, however, this kind of self-sacrificing person for the cause of Israel has not yet been created. He must be recruited from the teachers in the cities, seminaries, and the yeshivot supported by national community funds. One stipulation must be placed on every student who graduates from these institutions of learning: a minimum of one year must be spent, preferably with a decent salary, carrying out the instructions of this national apparatus to strengthen Jewish life. A well-organized, sincerely devoted leadership must be created with authority to place itself in the service of such an organization.

True, this will cost money, but who can point out a more vital or worthwhile purpose for expenditure than saving thousands of Jewish families from extinction? The time has come to make an accounting of our neglect.

Jewish public institutions and national religious bodies cannot afford to remain indifferent to the dangerous pressure of assimilation which threatens tens of thousands of Jews. Let us think of them every day rather than only in fund-raising campaigns. Let us activate every positive force for this effort against the torrent of assimilation. There is no greater or holier task of rescue for the Jewish future.

CHAPTER IX

MIXED MARRIAGES AND FAMILY TRAGEDIES

The family is society's most complex institution. Man and wife together, their mutual involvements and inter-relationships, the matters of livelihood, finances, children, friends, companionship—these are problems whose solution determines the success or failure of family life. Every family is subject to the unforeseen event, the unanticipated occurrence, which places in the balance its survival or collapse.

"And therefore shall a man leave his father and his mother and cleave unto his wife" (Genesis 2:24). The bond must be firmer than that which ties man to father and mother. God Himself, say our sages, is occupied with matchmaking: ". . . Said Rabbi Bar Hana, 'It is as difficult as the splitting of the Red Sea when the children of Israel crossed from Egypt'" (Moed Katan).

The Talmud tells us how complex it is to bring two people to dwell under the same roof and live out their years in peace.

"A Roman matron asked of Rabbi Jose ben Halafta: 'In how many days did the Holy One, praised be He, create the world?'

"'In six days.'

"'And from that time on until now what has He been doing?'

"'He joins couples, decreeing who should be married to whom.'

"'Is that all?', she asked. 'I too can do that. Many male and female slaves do I possess, and I can couple them in one hour.'

" 'Verily,' he replied, 'if it be a light matter in your eyes, with the Holy One it is as difficult as the splitting of the Red Sea.' He then left and went his way.

"What did she do? She brought one thousand male and female slaves, placed them in one row, and said to them, 'This one should be married to that one, and this one should be married to that one.' And thus she coupled them in one night.

"When the morning came they all came before her. This one had a fractured skull; the other had an eye gouged out; another had a broken arm; and another a fractured leg. This one said, 'I do not want to be married to this one.' And the other said, 'I do not want to be married to that one.'

"She at once sent for Rabbi Jose ben Halafta and said to him, 'My teacher, your Law is true, beautiful, and praiseworthy; you have spoken well' " (Vayikra Rabbah 8:1).

There are no two people on this earth of the same temperament or of identical character, habits, and thoughts. Every individual is a world to himself. For cohabitation of husband and wife to be harmonious and happy, what is required besides love, patience, and tolerance, is the ability to overlook one another's defects and errors. Even so no standard rules can be prescribed for the peaceful solution of family problems, for in no two families are the problems exactly alike. One must bear in mind the particular circumstances of the individuals involved.

Our sages likened the marriage of man and woman to the founding of a kingdom. The groom was compared to a king and the bride to a queen. Just as the state requires loyalty and patriotic devotion from its subjects and often the sacrifice of personal convenience for defense of the kingdom, husband and wife are likewise cautioned in their management of married life. They are urged to place the welfare and peace of the family higher than their own personal interest and comfort.

Even among the best and most peaceful families certain

problems are inevitable. Spats between husband and wife, bickering and minor tensions, are frequent. This is quite as it should be. Two people cannot agree in every particular at all times. Occasional squabbles are good for both sides; they make married life more interesting, if not stubbornly prolonged.

All this applies to a husband and wife whose union is based not only on love but who are of the same faith and same ethnic origin. The situation is quite different, however, when the marriage is mixed, when husband and wife are of different faiths and races.

Family problems in a couple of the same faith and national origin go no further than a spat or passing annoyance; when they happen to a mixed couple, there are bitter wrangles that often lead to an open rupture. The differences of character, temperament, and customs, inbred for generations, which are repressed in the days of courtship, erupt into an explosion in the moment of crisis. All that is needed is the slightest aspersion of the other's religion or race, and a violent conflict arises.

We know of cases where because of an innocent word, a casual charge of the kind that occurs in most families and would normally be forgotten, heated clashes have arisen which have wrecked the careers of man and wife, and ruined the lives of their children.

They had been married six years. He was the son of well reputed Jewish parents and she the daughter of a respectable Protestant family. They met at a dance and fell in love. The families were opposed to the match, but no force could keep them apart. She agreed to become a Jewess. A Reform rabbi carried out the conversion and performed the marriage. After a year a boy was born, and he was entered into the covenant of Abraham. In another year a daughter came. His father helped in setting up a business. The business prospered. They loved each other and lived in peace. There were small quarrels and difficulties, but they forgave and forgot. Their parents sometimes met at their home to compare notes on their grandchildren and to take pleasure in the idyllic happiness of their children.

One day she invited several non-Jewish friends to her home for an evening. Tea and refreshments were served. As ill luck had it the husband upset the teapot and spilled tea over the dress of one of his wife's friends. Amid the excitement the wife cried with some annoyance, "You damn Jew!"

Her husband left the company. His wife immediately regretted her words. When her friends left she excused herself; the insult had slipped out involuntarily. Her husband insisted that the expression stemmed from the concealed hatred she bore in her heart for all his people. The remarks grew stronger and words flew faster. Soon each was insulting the other's race and religion. Just as once there was no power to keep them apart, there was now no power to keep them together. Their home was broken up. The legal costs ruined his capital. The children remained with their mother, but without their father—broken souls.

Another case. The husband accused his wife of taking one drink too many at their social gatherings. Under the influence of alcohol he found that her behavior embarrassed him in the presence of friends. She made no denial. She did so— she argued—to soothe her overwrought nerves. Ever since she had married a "Jew boy," she had felt alone and forsaken by her family. This had the effect of a match on a vat of oil. Their passion was suddenly cooled. They stood facing one another like embittered enemies. Their life together was broken.

A wife once complained to me about her husband's odd behavior. "He goes around in a constant state of depression, doesn't say a word to me. Perhaps he's sorry he was converted and became a Jew. Perhaps he's ill. He has great respect for you and always speaks highly of you. Please help me. We can't go on this way much longer."

We sent for him and had an intimate conversation. He was quite disillusioned in his wife. He felt that she was unfaithful—she was cool to him. Perhaps it was due to his non-Jewish origin. Did he not practice Judaism as thoroughly as their friends who were Jews by birth?

We brought them together. The woman denied that she had been unfaithful. True, she had been cold to him, but this was because he was cold to her. Unwittingly the husband let slip a phrase about her mother's "Jewish interference." This distressed the wife greatly. "It's the gentile in you," she retorted. Nothing more was needed. There burst forth all the long-suppressed tensions based on their difference of origin. It was no longer a quarrel between husband and wife, but a bitter battle between two races and religions. By now reconciliation was out of the question. The husband applied for a divorce. Both children were strongly attached to the parents. The question of their custody was left to the judge. The husband returned to his family and their religious faith, and the wife to her parents. Not only did they ruin their own lives, but permanently disturbed the spiritual and emotional balance of their two innocent children.

When these incidents occur in the family life of unmixed couples, both Jewish and Christian, they are quarrels which in the main end in reconciliation. In mixed marriages, however, the difference is that relations are constantly on the verge of eruption. The slightest incident, the most trivial remark, wrecks domestic peace.

There are certain problems unique to mixed marriages. If the young man and woman had thought of them before the wedding they would have known enough to anticipate these problems. But the process of thought undergoes a total paralysis "in the state of love." The issues, therefore, are totally unexpected; they strike like a bolt from the blue and both husband and wife are uprooted and disoriented.

"We were teachers at the same high school," a couple told us. "We knew each other, fell in love. We were both of intellectual tastes, and broadminded and liberal in our outlook and convictions. Neither had much concern with religion." They had decided before the wedding that the children would be raised in the same spirit, without any religion. Later they were to make whatever choice pleased them.

During her pregnancy the wife's Jewish father asked that if the child be a boy, he be circumcised. Circumcision is recognized medically as a necessity for health purposes, and thousands of gentile children undergo the operation. However, this sorely disturbed the "liberal" non-Jewish father.

As it happened a daughter was born. However, the wife found it hard to forget or overlook her husband's attitude. She was disillusioned as to his liberalism. He was annoyed at her for ever having considered circumcision. Trifles in daily routine now began to disturb them. As intelligent people, they had enough insight to recognize that they could not attain happiness together. They gave up their home, and for all practical purposes the marriage was dissolved.

Their parents were originally from Lithuania. They had worked indefatigably to give their children the best possible education. Their son had completed a medical course with high distinction. His parents were happy. He entered a Catholic hospital as interne and there fell in love with a nurse. His parents' prayers and tears were of no avail—his only reaction was "I love her; she is my happiness." The fact that her parents were Catholics did not concern him. He did not believe in his own religion—what possible concern could the religion of his fiancée's parents be to him? He could not be held responsible for his parents' superstitions. "A man's a man for a' that," whether Jewish, Catholic, Protestant, or Moslem. As a doctor he knew that all men were biologically the same irrespective of religion.

The couple married and settled in a middle-sized provincial city. He became a successful practitioner. Constantly preoccupied with his practice, he did not notice how his home was becoming Catholicized. His children attended the Catholic parish school.

One day they returned in tears. Their schoolmates had been calling them ugly names, taunting them for their Jewish origin. Something stirred in the doctor's emotions. He opened his eyes. He began to notice that the corners of the rooms were filled with statues and crucifixes. He forbade his children to attend the Catholic school. His wife resisted, and in the ensuing argument she mentioned that she did not want her children to grow up into what their schoolmates had called them. This was the last straw. They left their fine home and applied for a divorce. The judge ruled that the children were to go with their mother. This completely shook the doctor. Feelings of guilt and remorse gnawed at his mind and heart. He became depressed, neglected his professional practice, and finished in a mental hospital.

In mixed unions husband and wife are exposed to unexpected difficulties and conflicts. The centuries old differences which both sides have inherited in one form or another, through a word or incident, are bound to upset and destroy the family's domestic bliss.

There is no power on earth which can erase the psychological difference between Jew and non-Jew, the legacy each has inherited with his mother's milk.

When sexual desire has been satisfied, at the first hostile occasion, inevitable in any family, the religious and ethnic differences reveal themselves. All at once, completely spontaneously, a fire is lit between husband and wife. The former loving couple fight like the bitterest enemies. In their hearts there springs an impulse to outdo each other in taunts about each other's faith and origin. Their domestic life is vitiated, the home collapses, their lives and the lives of their children are undermined.

CHAPTER X

CONVERTS AND THE PROSELYTIZING RABBIS

When the Children of Israel left Egypt, Scripture tells us, "A mixed multitude went up with them." According to Rashi this multitude consisted of converts, Egyptians who, impressed by the miracles wrought by Moses and Aaron, joined the exiles to wander with them in the wilderness and serve the God of the Israelites.

The children of Israel got no moment's respite or satisfaction from this group. They were the first to grumble, the first to incite disaffection and rebellion, and they constantly provoked the Israelites to mutiny against God. It was the evil-doing of the mixed multitude whom Moses—contrary to God's wish—had permitted to mix with the Israelites, that aroused the Lord's anger.

Divine Providence was aware that their going over to the Jewish camp was not based on acceptance of the faith of the Hebrews or the God of Abraham, but on "the flocks and herds and great amount of cattle." It was for this reason that the Almighty did not agree with Moses' plan for absorbing the Egyptian converts.

On the third day after the departure from Egypt they saw that the Israelites "cried out to the Lord" (Exodus 14) and prayed to the God of Abraham, Isaac, and Jacob. The multitude, however, complained to Moses: "Is it because there are no graves in Egypt that Thou hast taken us away to die in the wilderness? What is this which Thou hast done to us to bring us forth out of Egypt?" (Exodus 14:11). The miracles the multitude had seen Moses and Aaron perform in Egypt, the crossing of the Red Sea, the victorious war against

Amalek, the dropping of the manna, the miracle of the quails
—none of these was able to dispel their strongly rooted
belief in the Egyptian divinities. At the first opportunity,
when Moses lingered on Mount Sinai longer than expected,
and the converts observed the Israelites disturbed and their
faith in God and in Moses shaken, the grip of the old idols
of Egypt regained its hold. They gathered around Aaron,
threatening him with death, and said, "Up, make us gods
that shall go before us; for of this man Moses that hath
brought us up out of the land of Egypt, we know not what
is become of him" (Exodus 32).

Our sages comment on this passage: "And the Lord spake
unto Moses: Go get thee down, for thy people which thou
hast brought up out of the land of Egypt hath become corrupt." The sages say, "The Pentateuch passage does not say
'the people' or 'my people,' but specifies 'thy people.' " From
this it can be deduced that God said to Moses, "The multitude which thou hast drawn into the fold of Israel against
my wish saying that it is good that the heathen should know
of My Presence—these have led the people of Israel to corruption."

The mixed multitude brought about the debasement of
the Israelites. They incited them to deny the God of their
forefathers and to build the Golden Calf. When the calf
was erected the multitude shouted to the Hebrews in deri-
sion, "Behold, the God of Israel!" Our sages say that God
said to Moses, "I bade thee take My people out, but in doing
so thou hast taken into thy fold those of whom thou sayest,
'It is good that they turn to God'; I have prophesied what
these are capable of doing."

Because of this our sages prohibited us to take proselytes.
They are an evil excrescence upon the body of Israel. Evil
will fall upon him who makes converts (Jebamot 29).

It is impossible, say our wise men, for a person to alter
his particular religious origins. With extremely few exceptions a man cannot, even wishing to do so, pour the blood
from his veins and transfer it into new arteries as though it

were water. No matter how a person may change his ideals, views, and traditions, he remains essentially what he was when he was a child. This is why our sages declared, "Most proselytes return to their origin for the most trivial reasons and their behavior seduces the Jews" (Kiddushin 80).

For this reason we have rarely had missionaries to propagate our faith among other peoples. We never sought to convince others to accept our doctrines and to live according to our Torah and the interpretations of the sages. On the contrary, we adopted the doctrine of the prophet Micah: "For all people will walk every one in the name of his god, and we will walk in the name of the Lord our God for ever and ever" (Micah 4:5). We hope and pray that the time will come when "the world will be perfected," convinced of the truth of our Torah, but until that day we practise the prophetic doctrine of letting "each walk in the way of his god" while ourselves walking in the path of ours.

When a gentile comes to be converted we traditionally dissuade him with the queries, "Where hast thou seen such that thou comest to be converted? Dost thou not know that the people of Israel are persecuted and despised, and great troubles are put upon them? Why should you assume the yoke and burden of Jewishness?" When the gentile replies that he knows all this, but that out of a deep conviction of the truth of Judaism he is willing to endure humiliation and sorrow, he is then taught the essential articles of faith, the commandments, duties, practices, and laws of the Jewish religion. If the convert accepts the entire yoke of the faith but cavils at a single commandment prescribed in the Torah, he is not brought into the community of Israel. This is the age-old manner prescribed for the reception of proselytes.

There have been converts in all periods of history, but these were gere tzedek (righteous proselytes), men of deep character and of profound faith who were drawn to Judaism by the light of its Torah. Out of a great spiritual thirst they drank deeply from the fountain of Jewish faith, strengthened by their firm belief in the one indivisible God. These converts were honest and sincere idealists ready to make any sacrifice for Judaism. Many of them died as martyrs, and they remain in Jewish tradition as legendary saints whose name is remembered with a blessing.

Converts who have accepted Judaism for personal reasons, to improve their economic state, to marry a Jew or Jewess, or to attain some personal ambition, have never been accepted into the Jewish fold as true converts. They have inspired no confidence, since they did not come to us out of love for the God of Israel and the community of Israel but out of self-interest. If later it should pay them to become something else they would not hesitate to change again.

Converts of this type have never been an asset to us. In countless cases, they have turned out unprincipled adventurers. After joining the flock of Israel, they misled our sons and daughters like the Egyptian converts. As for the "righteous proselytes"—those who adopted Judaism from pure conviction and out of love for the God of Israel—these have been few in number. They were individuals of great stature, restless, inquiring souls searching for a belief, a credo that would satisfy their ranging spirits. They finally attained the true depth of Judaism to give them "peace of mind," becoming scholars, sages, and saints.

The converts who came to Judaism out of opportunism eventually reverted to their origins. Their children married gentiles, their grandchildren frequently became anti-Semites, professing openly the hatred the grandfathers had concealed in their hearts.

One need not be a psychologist to know that what people do not accept with goodwill but from outward circumstances or pressure will arouse a hidden resentment that in time develops into hatred of the circumstances that impelled the change. This cumulative resentment is passed on to the descendants.

In the presence of a convert's descendant even to the tenth generation, it is forbidden to embarrass him by mentioning his gentile origin, says a passage in Rashi (Exodus

18). This applies to a proselyte converted from personal motives, for marriage purposes, one actually devoid of any religious feeling. This insincerity is transferred to his children, and descendants unto the tenth generation may be offended by a remark about non-Jews in their presence.

Our sages maintain that those who convert "out of fear of being killed by wild beasts or driven by bad dreams, or in anticipation of the world's end" are not true proselytes. In the days of King Solomon the Hebrews were opposed to taking converts, for they suspected the conversions were politically motivated—to become allies of Israel and use its power and prestige.

This negative attitude to proselytes has always been the Jewish position, not on biological or racial grounds, but because our sages held that no man can root out of his soul what he imbibed in his mother's milk.

It is also the belief of our sages that many Jewish practices are specifically Jewish in nature; they are carried over from one generation to the next, and are peculiar to those who are of Jewish birth and upbringing.

Recently Jewish life has seen an astonishing change in relation to proselytes. Instead of posing the traditional question, "What hast thou seen that draws thee hither?" and dissuading him from the step, the convert is encouraged by rabbis (both Reform and others). A Jewish youth or girl falls in love with a non-Jew. They need only come to the rabbi and tell him they love each other and he will put himself completely at their disposal. If the Jewish parents are opposed, the rabbi will persuade them to agree to the match, providing the bride or groom is willing to be converted— despite the fact that according to rule such are not accounted as proselytes—"A man who is converted because of a woman, and a woman who is converted because of a man—these are not proselytes" (Jebamot 24).

There are even rabbis (orthodox as well as Reform) who announce publicly that among the functions in which they specialize is conversion to Judaism! There are rabbis (and rabbanim) who lay claim to be philosophers and theologians. They have found reasons for "special allowances" in cases which far greater religious authorities have been unable to resolve. They use "practical sense" in their profession in fields where they have never filled any authoritative role. They know and understand all. As an American-trained rabbi once told me, "Joshua, Akiba, Gamaliel were rabbis, and I too am a rabbi". . . . They pontificate with the full authority of their own Shulchan Arukh, on what is important and what is not, what may and what must be deleted from the Jewish laws in keeping with "the modern outlook."

In the opinion of these rabbis, Judaism, which gave the world a faith and a living God, has become antiquated. It does not fit our twentieth century civilization. Therefore they create their own laws and customs. They are the self-appointed arbiters, and have no need to consult halakhic authority. The only authority is the rabbi himself. Tradition follows the Minhag America (American practice).

Each rabbi is a law to himself. He creates his own Torah, with his own articles of faith and his own directives on how to adapt Judaism, its laws and traditions, to the free democratic life such as happens to please the members of his congregation.

With these rabbis, Judaism has become like the manna the children of Israel ate in the wilderness. It has whatever taste the eater likes best. It is a supermarket where one can choose from the great variety offered. If the rabbi feels that something is inconvenient for his members, no tabu or injunction can prevail—it is annulled as not in keeping with the spirit of our age.

These rabbis have contributed to the spread of mixed marriages. Because of their easy conversions, they have become common. Years ago such unions were confined to the so-called aristocratic circles. In recent years, because of the "new theology" trimming and streamlining Judaism and the encouragement given applicants for conversion, mixed marriages have spread like an epidemic.

These religious leaders who are so lenient to the demands of their membership and who make compromises in fundamental Jewish law and practice in order to keep domestic peace in their congregations, are not leaders, but are themselves led by the nose. The lay membership decides what is forbidden and what is permissible, and the rabbis accept their decisions as final and authoritative.

These converting rabbis offer the following excuses: if no conversion were effected the couple would still marry and the offspring would be raised as gentiles. This is merely to justify the cavalier attitude of Reconstructionist Judaism to the essential laws of our faith—a justification that brings Jewish families to the brink of extinction.

In most mixed marriages, after the non-Jewish spouse has been converted, the Jewish family intermingles with non-Jewish families and eventually is lost. Of those who do make a pretense at maintaining Judaism (of the common North American variety) the children grow up in a state of limbo—neither Jews nor gentiles.

If rabbis and rabbanim were to resolve firmly not to practise conversion for marriage purposes, this would have a great psychological effect on Jewish youth, and cause them to think twice before engaging in marital overtures to non-Jews.

The behavior of our rabbis causes us distress and sorrow. They persuade the parents (who have perforce agreed to the union) that the conversion of a non-Jewish bride or groom is a gain for the improvement of "public relations" and "goodwill" between the two faiths, as well as a gain for Judaism and the Jewish family. Sometimes when it happens that the new convert adopts Jewish practices for a short while after the wedding, rabbi and parents feel quite proud. They publicly praise the qualities of the new member of their household and tell all their friends. This has had the effect among families with no mixed marriages or converted Christians among their relatives, of making them feel the lack of "pedigree lineage" in their family trees.

This feeling stems from the lowered level of American Jewish moral standards. When before have Jews taken pride in non-Jewish ancestry or family relationship—even when the convert in truth followed Judaism? Among certain Jewish parents, a proselyte daughter-in-law who can make tasty *gefillte fish* for the Sabbath and *kreplach* for the festivals is more highly regarded than their own daughters and certainly more than their Jewish daughters-in-law. In the presence of these parents not a word must be spoken against mixed marriages.

Another reason by these rabbis is that the Torah bids us love the convert. But these proselytizing rabbis must realize that their interpretation of the passage is a distortion, and only a justification for their own guilt feelings.

The Torah's precept is applied only to converts who come to Judaism out of religious conviction and who volunteer to assume the yoke of the Law and commandments, the righteous proselytes. To such one is obliged to show love.

Most converts today, however, undergo conversion out of personal interest, i. e., for the love of a Jewish youth or girl. According to Jewish law they are not righteous proselytes or true converts. The conversion may make them no longer gentile but does not turn them into Jews. They hang in the limbo between Jew and gentile. With few exceptions their children and grandchildren marry gentiles and in time they disappear totally from the Jewish community.

We are acquainted with a proselyte, an intelligent person who underwent conversion to marry a beautiful Jewish girl. He observed Jewish ritual in its entirety. In the evenings after work he studied the prayers and blessings and learned how to read and write Hebrew. He came to daily services every morning, clothed in the traditional prayershawl and phylacteries. He was called to the reading of the Torah, pronounced the benedictions for the Torah by heart, kept the Sabbath, observed the laws of kashruth, sang the Sabbath melodies at the *Shalosh-seudot,* and sent his children to the Talmud Torah. His parents-in-law were extremely

proud of him, and told their friends about his Jewish qualities and how young Jews could take a lesson from him on
how to follow the traditional Jewish way of life. This was
responsible for a great increase in intermarriage. In these
marriages all non-Jewish partners were converted, but not
all lived as Jews—as Abraham the son of Abraham (the
name acquired by all male converts to Judaism).

One day, quite without warning, Abraham stopped attending synagogue, started working on the Sabbath, and his children left the Talmud Torah. The reasons are not important.
"Abraham ben Abraham" returned to the ways of his parents,
became an active member of his parents' church, his children married Christians, and today Abraham ben Abraham's
grandchildren are complete gentiles.

Recently a number of Reform rabbis made an attempt at
a convention to reverse all the laws about converts and conversion. As we know, Reform recognizes no mitzvot or pro-
hibitions of the Torah to be observed and followed. Their
faith is more Unitarian than Jewish. The constant preaching of Reform rabbis about the beauty of Christianity and
prophetic universalism has led their members to outright
assimilation and in many cases to apostasy. These who seek
Judaism find no satisfaction either in their temples or in
their form of Judaism. Now these rabbis have appealed for
Jews to become missionaries. They have begun a campaign
to turn gentiles into Jews and to bring them into their
temples. Their booklet on becoming a Jew does not even
require circumcision. All that is needed is for the applicant
to attend lectures on Judaism an hour a day for several
weeks. Later on a ceremony is prepared and in the presence
of a number of Reform rabbis the convert is given a biblical
name. He is sworn in as a member of the community of Israel
and receives a certificate stating that he is a Jew.

A Reform rabbi recently stated that from a religious point
of view he saw no reason why a Jew could not marry a Christian. There might be objections from a practical point of
view but these were no different from the practical objec-

tions brought against marriages between Catholics and Protestants.

The *American Israelite,* a weekly put out by the Reform element, published a large photograph of a Christian-Jewish wedding couple, indicating that a Reform rabbi had solemnized the marriage together with a minister. The wedding took place in a church. When a weekly which assumes itself a rabbinical publication publicizes a mixed marriage so prominently and captions it "Rabbi and Clergyman Perform Wedding Together" it encourages other youth to follow suit. This is called Judaism and these sponsors of apostasy are called "rabbis."

Ever since we became a nation we have known rabbis to be those who devote themselves to the study and interpretation of the commandments and rules of the Torah. Today there are people calling themselves rabbis who apply themselves to breaking the commandments of the Torah and who seek reasons to justify its most serious breaches.

Could such a thing occur among other faiths? Would a religious leader lead a member of his congregation into another creed?

Mixed marriages are the end result of assimilation and the beginning of the Christianization process. Mixed marriages performed in a church by a rabbi and a clergyman are nothing more or less than apostasy.

Rabbis, great religious authorities, who for generations have wrestled with the problems of Jewish law, long ago laid down the precept that conversions for the purpose of marriage "must not be performed." Now rabbis set up their own rules which meet the convenience of their membership, as they say, "in harmony with modern times." They introduce non-Jewish, disintegrative influences into the Jewish camp, bring about tragic conflict between parent and child, cause mental divisions in the minds of children, bring about spiritual bankruptcy.

In a remarkable letter published in the National Jewish Post a learned and pious Christian named Dr. Anton Sanglo writes about the Anglo-Jewish writers and rabbis whose articles do not show enough respect for Jewish laws, customs, and traditions. "I feel," he asserts, "that one of the main reasons for Jew-baiting and anti-Semitism is the apologetic attitude and inferiority complex of many Jews, unfortunately of many of their leaders, which expresses itself in a tasteless profanation and burlesquing of their own most sacred customs and traditions in their foolish attempt, like frightened sheep, to make themselves look like the majority as much as possible."

When Ezra the Scribe returned to Judaea with the exiles from Babylon, he purged the land of idolatry and assimilation and restored the Mosaic Torah to the Jews. He revived the laws and practices of their forefathers and sharply rebuked those who had taken Babylonian wives. He cried out, "Ye have transgressed and have taken strange wives to increase the trespass of Israel. Now, therefore, make confession unto the Lord God of your fathers and do his pleasure: and separate yourselves from the people of the land and from the strange wives" (Ezra 10:11).

The greatest and most important act of Ezra's day was his cleansing Jewish family life of mixed marriage. This act should be repeated today. Mixed marriages were always accounted the last stage towards apostasy. "They turn no more to the ways of Jeshurun." All the rabbis and rabbanim who practise conversion and help spread the evil of mixed marriage must confess their past sins against the Jewish people and against the God of Israel; in the words of Ezra, "I am ashamed and blush to lift up my face to Thee, my God, for our iniquities are increased over our head and our trespass is grown up into the heavens. . . . Here we are before Thee in our guilt though none can stand before Thee —because of this" (Ezra 9:6, 15).

CHAPTER XI

OIL AND WATER

Mixed Marriage and the Tragedy of the Children

Mixed marriage is not only an agonizing Jewish problem —it is one felt keenly by the Christian denominations. Like the Jews, both Protestant and Catholic faiths are strongly opposed thereto, and place all sorts of obstacles in its way. These religions, like Judaism, see in mixed marriage not only the problems of living together, which so often comes to a tragic end for both sides, but also as the greatest threat to the continuity of their religious communities and their individual codes of conduct.

The Jewish point of view, firmly established in the days of our forefathers, is expressed in the Torah as an unequivocal prohibition. When Shechem ben Hamor abducted and raped Dinah, daughter of Jacob, and was later ready to fulfill all the conditions of the sons of Jacob to get their consent to his marriage, the sons replied to Hamor with firmness; "We cannot do this thing—to give our sister to one that is uncircumcised; for that would be a reproach unto us" (Genesis 34). This is the unambiguous and strict prohibition in the Torah. The reason is given on the spot: "Neither shalt thou make marriage with them—thy daughter thou shalt not give unto his son, nor his daughter shalt thou take unto thy son" (Deuteronomy 7). Mixed marriages eventually lead to alienation from the God of Israel and the people of Israel.

The Jewish religion has clearly defined rules, procedures, and "hedges," which in the course of history have proven eminently reasonable and sensible, and which saved our

111

people from physical and spiritual extinction. At certain periods, various commandments and "hedges" were modified. But this remained an iron-clad rule which was at no time altered by anyone, since mixed marriages were always considered equivalent to apostasy, and those who entered into them were like lepers placed beyond the pale.

Apostasy—it is hard to imagine a word more pregnant with revulsion and horror for Jews. It means not only putting an end to Jews and Judaism, but a complete break with one's family, with one's whole past, with the future of the Jewish people. For a Jew to be baptized means that he has left his people, and erased himself completely from Adath Israel.

It is true that at this moment we have little to fear from any apostasy epidemic among the Jews of this continent. The motives—economic, political, and the rest, as they once existed in Europe—are lacking. The realistic observer, however, beholds not only the present, but the total picture. In the constant and widespread intermarriage epidemic he sees the last act of a process of disintegration in our Jewish life, leading to the same end as apostasy.

We have among us "Israel-will-not-perish" Jews, the perpetual Pollyanna optimists. Their practice is always to minimize every latent threat. Even when deep within they recognize the symptoms of the danger to come, they cover their heads with the cloak of optimism. They prefer to denounce the warnings as exaggerated, hysterical, and unfounded. Were they aware of the sad experiences of the last three decades, and were they to draw the necessary conclusions, it would be as clear to them as it is to us that the epidemic of mixed marriages is the beginning of the end for the Jew.

Mixed marriage is a matter that touches a basic precept of the Jewish faith. When a Jewish girl marries a non-Jew, or when a Jewish youth takes a Christian girl, they have cut through a fence which for millennia has protected our family life and preserved the Jewish people from decline. Mixed marriages are a cause of distress not only when they occur

in observant Jewish families, but also when they strike the
so-called "secular" Jews, even those who are far from religious or national Jewish life. Secularist Jews know and
feel just as religious Jews do—that mixed marriages, being
in the main unsuccessful and ending in collapse, are the
cause of parental grief over a son or daughter totally estranged from family and Jewish roots. It is an instinct deeply
implanted, that the generations to come should be Jewish.
They have ground to doubt whether their son or daughter
will remain Jewish. They can be fairly sure that the children
will not be Jews.

In a mixed marriage there exists not only the difference
of religious identification, but even more, there is the spiritual abyss between two peoples, with different personalities,
characteristics, mentalities. Mixed marriage is a clash of
opposing worlds. As soon as the first flush of love passes,
the domestic peace explodes. Mixed marriages are like oil
and water. The inevitable antagonisms will come to the
surface, and lead to scandal, embitterment, separation.

Studies by sociologists and specialists in human relations
indicate that most such unions are unhappy. The difficulties
that stem from religious beliefs, customs, specific habits and
practices, cannot be foreseen during courtship, as leading
to conflict and disappointment.

For three decades we have been studying the family life
of intermarried couples, and we have found most tragic
failures. The stubborn characters who make a public show
of their success in marriage and declare they have no regrets,
repress their inner anxieties, bemoan their fate in silence,
and do their best to keep their own families from disintegration.

The home atmosphere is one without intimacy. No sooner
does one cross the threshold than one feels that two distinct
people of differing character and customs dwell there. Even
among those who have achieved a greater degree of adjustment, one senses that family peace is based on mutual
tolerance rather than on deep love.

Psychiatrists and students who devote themselves to problems of family life state that adaptability in married life is a highly delicate and complex process even when the couple stems from families of the same environment. But when the canvas on which a couple must delineate its future is material of another race or faith, the prospect for a successful wedded life is remote.

After the wedding, when sexual desires are stilled and the flame of love is cooled, there enters the feeling of companionship and respect, dependent on the understanding they have with each other. Each must tolerate and have patience for the other. But a person's patience can crack when sorely tried by a trifle—all of life, after all, is a succession of trifles. A tense incident arises, an angry exchange of words takes place—this kind of contretemps occurs among the best behaved couples.

Experience has shown that among couples of separate religions and nationalities, there is seldom any appreciable respect or tolerance. In a sharp exchange of words, an expression escapes, a derogatory word which slurs a race or faith. Nothing can avoid this; nothing can make up for it. Husband or wife has a rude awakening, and sees the great error that has been made. Minds begin to function clearly; they realize the grief which they have caused their parents and family. They feel the barrier in race and religion their youthful love had covered with an opaque veil.

Neither can longer live together in peace under the same roof. There is no way back. Their hearts, once filled with love, are now poisoned with hatred. It is not the hatred of two individuals, but a long-drawn-out historic enmity. Their personal problems have become a conflict between nationalities. The accusations are laid to the account of the character, customs, manners of the race, and the results are tragic for both.

It is even more tragic when a couple has had offspring. Conflicts spring up around the children. Father and mother both want the child, but not merely as parents do. Each feels that the one who has the child can raise it in his or her own beliefs. The antipathy is more than personal, but collective. Often it remains for the court to decide in whose care the children are to be raised.

We were once visited by a woman of middle height, strikingly beautiful, who sobbed as she spoke. She told us her story and asked for advice.

"I was born and raised in a small town in the West. My parents were freethinkers. I saw no Jewish life in my home and received no Jewish training. It happened quite naturally that I fell in love with a Christian young man, member of a prominent family.

"I knew my father and mother were Jews, but beyond that I had no connection with Jewishness and Judaism. It therefore came as a great surprise when my parents showed strong resistance to my marriage. The parents of the Christian young man likewise opposed it. However, we loved each other and married without asking consent.

"A year after the wedding a boy was born; we were very happy. Two years passed and I bore a girl. In the fourth year, I noticed that my husband was becoming a stranger to me. For every trifle he uttered accusations and insults. I remained silent. A rumor came to my ears that my husband was carrying on an affair. I didn't want to believe it. I loved him and it could not be true. Once, in a moment of friendly conversation, I mentioned with a smile that such a rumor was making the rounds.

"He froze immediately; then became excited. I tried to appease his anger, telling him that I put no credence in it. I could not calm him. When I approached him, he shouted in my face, 'Away from me, you filthy Jewess!'

"I awoke suddenly. 'What did you say?' I asked, not wanting to believe my ears. He repeated with even greater venom, 'You filthy Jewess!' My eyes were opened; suddenly I recovered my sobriety. I left with my two children and went to my parents. After difficulty and scandal I obtained a divorce. I settled down in a large Jewish community, got a job, worked my way up as an executive in a large business. My children attend Talmud Torah. I want to give them a good Jewish education. My former husband, learning that the children were being raised as Jews, has lost all interest in them. This is how I saddened my younger years. It isn't only my fault. It is also the fault of my freethinking parents who conducted a non-Jewish home and a pagan life.

"I came to you for two reasons. My boy is not circumcised and I want to see that it is done, as I wish him to be a complete Jew. Tell my story so that others will perhaps be able to take a lesson."

For others to take a lesson?

When a young couple of differing religions are in love, no talk, no reasoning will help. They are deaf to words; no one can convince them that their differing backgrounds will be an obstacle to their happiness.

There are those who claim to be non-religious and are married by a civil ceremony. They too risk their happiness. They think that without a religion, not belonging to either denomination, they will succeed in avoiding family discord. A fatal error. In time, especially when children come, the age-old religious instinct awakens either in the husband or wife—to give the child some kind of identity. The question then arises: What kind of education for the child? To what community is he to be attached?

After all, he cannot grow up in a vacuum, without identity. If there are such "unclassified" persons they are rare individuals. Even the non-religious know that they have their roots and belonging in some national community. But in what category are the children of such parents? With what community can they be identified?

There are no "neutral" or unspecified "Canadian" or "American" children. They also realize that a child cannot be raised in two religions—to choose one of them later when he is fully grown. What the mixed couple refuses to see when they are in love becomes clear later; children cannot be reared minus an environment, neither as Jews nor as gentiles. If they are sufficiently intelligent, especially if they still love each other and do not wish to offend each other's feelings, they must face the complex question: What kind of education? They feel the full tragedy not only of their children's problems, but their own as well. No matter how they maintain the status quo in the home, each senses the wall which stands between them.

When Sunday comes in the provincial cities most of the neighbors attend church, and send their children off to Sunday school. The child sees that his parents remain at home, but he asks that he be allowed to do as his playmates—he too wants to go.

At first the parents are silent. They try to humor the child and talk themselves out of the situation. Later when the child grows older he realizes the differing origins of his parents. Then he asks the cutting, "Dad, you are a Jew, Mom is a gentile. What am I?"

Intermarried couples, of course, should have anticipated this question. Were they not forewarned of the conflicts which intermarriage brings? Nevertheless, the child's question comes as a shock. They are confused, try to avoid giving an answer. Some inner fear inhibits them. The atmosphere of the home becomes strained. The child's question has placed a wedge between the parents. His child's instinct perceives the alienation and estrangement. He becomes a split person with a split soul—does not know to which nationality and religion he belongs.

We know of a mixed marriage where the wife is an intelligent gentile. Because of her love for a Jew she formally adopted Judaism. She practises her adopted faith to the best of her ability. Her children attend Hebrew School. Her son had an imposing bar mitzvah and was a member of the junior congregation. The parents of both husband and wife are still living and are visited by their children and families. The husband's parents are observant Jews and the wife's parents are pious Christians. Both sets of grandparents visit the couple regularly, but time their visits to avoid meeting each other. This is heart-breaking for their children, the mixed couple.

When the grandchildren visit their Jewish *zeydeh* and *bubbeh* they are Jewish children. When they are with their Christian grandparents, they are Christian. Their comrades of both faiths know they are children of a mixed marriage.

The expected, of course, eventually happened. A few high school chums were chatting. One after another they asked the boy the question, "Which are you—Jewish or gentile?"

The boy came home wounded and broken up. He bluntly put to his mother his school chums' query. Taken by surprise, she had no answer. The lad broke into hysterical sobbing, reproaching his mother: "Why didn't you marry one of your own, one of your own people? Didn't you give any thought to the children you'd be bringing into the world? I don't know what I am—Jew or Christian! To my Jewish grandparents I am a Jew; to my Christian grandparents, I am a Christian. Jewish girls treat me as though I were a gentile; gentile girls look on me as a Jew! What am I? Who am I? What on earth have you done?"

One who has written about the inner conflict in a child of mixed marriage is the well-known Jewish poet and publicist, Ephraim Auerbach, who dealt with it in his column in the New York *Morgen-Journal*. The caption read "Shmerl Esposito." It was a picture of a grotesque, incongruous side of our Jewish life in America. Like the old Greek actors our tragedy wears a double mask for two faces—each distorted. The youngster carries two nations on his little shoulders—incapable of fusing or harmonizing. The name "Shmerl" is after his mother's grandfather. "Esposito" is his Sicilian father's. The child is an imcomplete "Shmerl" and a fragmented "Esposito." His mother wants Shmerl to attend a Hebrew school, to know the Jewish festivals. On Friday evenings Shmerl goes to the synagogue in a clean white shirt, a *yarmulka* on his head. He echoes "Amen" to the kiddush, and chants the Sabbath hymns and tunes—"Shalom Aleichem" and "L'cha Dodi." On Friday nights he is a Jewish Shmerl—the incarnation of his namesake, Grandfather Shmerl.

On Sundays a complete reversal takes place. The Catholic

Esposito takes over his soul. His father, a devout churchgoer, takes little Shmerl Esposito with him to his devotions. What takes place is like the struggle in the womb of Mother Rebecca when she was bearing Jacob and Esau. The "Esposito" urge draws him to his father's church just as his mother exerts an equally strong pull in the other direction.

"Shmerl Esposito" is desperate and confused; his heart and soul are rent asunder. He doesn't know where to find his bearings; his security is gone. The child lives in constant fear of being cast off by one or other of the two elements which make him up. This is the result with most children of mixed marriage. Within them there develops bitter hostility toward their parents for having complicated and embittered their lives. No matter what kind of training the children are given, they sense the dichotomy which separates their parents' religions and ethnic origins. It is against nature to unite opposing and contrasting thoughts, faiths, ways of life.

Our observation has been that the majority of children of mixed marriages enter the non-Jewish fold. Their father's or mother's Jewishness remains a sort of superfluous afterthought, with considerable effect, albeit of a negative nature, on their characters. There develops a strong antipathy against the Jewish side of their ancestry—a feeling which often turns them into anti-Semites.

I once observed an experience of this type. It was in a small provincial town. The father was a Jew, the mother a Christian who had been converted to Judaism. They had two grown-up sons, both with the mark of Abraham. They had only rare contacts or friendship with Jewish children. Their mother bore a third son and a *mohel* was brought in from the big city. The Jews of the town, happy to participate, accompanied the mohel to the house to help conduct the ceremony. They were met at the door by the two grown sons, both with iron bars in their hands, who warned them not to enter, and threatened any who would dare bring upon their new-born brother the mark of shame already cut into their own bodies. When along with their father we appealed to them to avoid a scandal, they exploded in complete anger against their father, calling him ugly names, and insulting him and reviling the Jewish people and faith.

What other names are there for these children but anti-Semites and renegades? As mentioned, sprinkling of baptismal water is not a prerequisite for apostasy—every mixed marriage leads directly and inevitably to the same end.

Among Jews, apostasy (*sh'mad*) means not merely abandoning the Jewish religion for another; it means literally, annihilation, extinction.

"Forget not the day of thy death," our sages have cautioned. Jewish survival will not be assured on this continent if we shut our eyes and ignore the fatal threat which hovers over us—the kiss of death, mixed marriage.

CHAPTER XII

MIXED MARRIAGES IN JEWISH LIFE TODAY

In the days before the Children of Israel stood before Mount Sinai, before they were chosen a nation of priests and a holy people, two dangers threatened their future—one physical and the other spiritual. Since they were an unprotected minority surrounded by foes, the danger of physical destruction was serious and menacing. The Egyptians wanted to do away with the able Israelites, who were a thorn in their side.

The second danger was this. The Israelites had lived among the Egyptians for centuries and knew the Egyptian way of life, religion, and civilization. They might well imitate these ways, mix with them, and eventually be swallowed up.

Our sages say the Children of Israel were saved from the Egyptians by virtue of four things:

a) they did not change their tongue;
b) they did not change their names;
c) they did not utter aloud their private secrets;
d) they did not transgress sexually with the Egyptians.

God redeemed them because they struggled against Egyptian influence and held fast to their ancestral traditions.

This is why the Exodus from Egypt is the focus of our faith and our history. In the Five Books of Moses, the Prophets, the later Scriptures, in almost every traditional prayer, "Remember the going out from Egypt" is constantly mentioned; for the life of the Israelites in Egypt is the proving stone of Jewish history, symbolizing the future historical stages of Jewish life among the peoples of the world.

Which of the two dangers—the physical or the spiritual—

is a greater threat to Jewish survival? Our sages considered
them equally dangerous. "How can this people exist among
the nations?" they asked in wonderment. It was difficult to
grasp how we had managed to survive in spite of the horrors
of persecution. This phenomenon had no counterpart in history. The only explanation they could offer was that the nation's survival was guaranteed by Divine Providence through
miraculous mediation.

In the long range account, it is quite probable that assimilation, mixed marriage, and conversion have made more inroads
than physical persecution.

When we look at Jewish history we are faced with a puz-
zling fact. In the countries where Jews enjoy political and
economic security and are not disturbed in their religious
and cultural rights, Jewish spiritual life becomes looser and
weaker. The impetus to assimilate with the non-Jewish majority becomes stronger. If, however, there is a threat of
physical peril from without, Jewish continuity is no problem
at all. External oppression has always brought to life those
creative forces which strengthen and solidify internal Jewish
life. The emancipation, on the other hand, has in most countries introduced currents of self-negation and assimilation.

Our task here is not to analyze these facts. We are merely
stating the axiom that where Jews suffer no physical danger
there is great risk of a spiritual breakdown. Today assimilation, mixed marriage, and estrangement from Jewish life
threaten Jewish survival more than persecution and pogroms.

Remarkably, the means used to ward off physical attack
has generally been a spiritual one. When tyrants issued de-
crees to strip Jews of their human rights, their defense lay in
their own moral and spiritual strength. When we were compelled to seek refuge in another country, it was Jewish willingness to sacrifice, the feeling that "God will not forsake his
people," that gave us strength and courage in our darkest mo-
ments. We clung to our religious-national individuality. Every
detail of Jewish life was governed by law, and we constituted
ourselves an autonomous spiritual state.

With Emancipation and the Enlightenment a great change has overwhelmed us. Instead of fortifying our inner resistance, always our best weapon, our defense is now carried on only one front. Our energy is directed against the external foe seeking to suppress us politically, socially, and economically. The spiritual danger to our existence is overlooked, and the destructive disease of mixed marriage is ignored.

We have established national organizations with vast personnel and apparatus whose budgets extend to the millions, for the purpose of warding off anti-Semitic attack. We have created "goodwill" movements, non-sectarian organizations, Christian and Jewish alliances, interfaith associations, which consume Jewish time, energy, and money, all for the purpose of convincing non-Jews that we are as good as anyone else, and to refute the anti-Semites.

We have no desire to minimize the importance of these activities, though we do have reservations about the results achieved. We will say, however, that if the same effort, energy, and money were used for inner strengthening, to combat assimilation, mixed marriages, and self-estrangement, we could boast a greater and more positive achievement. These national organizations engaged mainly in apologetics, are constantly "interpreting" us to the non-Jewish world, to prove the arguments of the anti-Semites false and libelous, the disease of psychically maladjusted persons. They simply do not see the plain truth: our own Jewish world is in flames and on the verge of collapse; branches of Israel are not blossoming, and the roots are drying up.

The paradox continues; when the physical and economical life of Jews is secure, the tendency toward dissolution and self-negation is most threatening. Since most Jews live in countries where there is no danger of physical attack, the spiritual peril has increased. The trend to assimilation grows from day to day.

This is not usually a conscious process. An individual will cast off Jewish duties and responsibilities without understanding what he does. Traditional barriers are sloughed off, the

Jewish home is equated with the non-Jewish, and thus the thread which bound us to our glorious past is severed.

It is a process which does not consciously substitute a different culture for Judaism; it is not based on conviction, but on the "easy way," the path of least resistance—a convenient escape from responsibilities and duties. It makes the Jew something that is no longer a Jew, yet not a gentile—a vagrant wandering in a spiritual limbo without a home.

We had hoped that creation of a Jewish state would set aflame a new and positive attitude to our faith and ideals. It has proved an illusion.

It is a sad fact that after creation of the State, when new lustre was added to the Jewish name and Jewish security gained in the lands of the dispersion, the trend towards assimilation also rose. The flight from Judaism assumed serious proportions and the number of mixed marriages increased. It is possible that Jewish responsibility was weakened through confidence that Israel had solved the problem of Jewish national existence, and Jews might now indulge in the luxury of freeing themselves of the bothersome yoke.

The transition to the Church has become a phenomenon not confined to frightened and confused German Jews or fugitives from Nazism, but one which occurs among Jews born and raised in the free countries.

We cannot ignore the network the Christian Scientists have spread in American Jewish society; a considerable number of Jews have been ensnared by friends and acquaintances by the missionary zeal of Christian sectarian fanaticism.

There are no exact statistics. But the greater evil is intermarriage. The facts and figures we mention come from published reports and authoritatively informed individuals. In an essay on the number of Jews in the world today Jacob Lestchinsky writes (in *Folk Un Velt*, published by the World Jewish Congress) that waves of assimilation are inundating Jewish life in the diaspora. They are undermining the basis of Jewish national existence. Mixed marriages that in effect lead to apostasy in the second generation are on the upswing.

Recently there have been alarms not only from small Jewish communities but from the large centers. The Jewish press in England reports with great concern an epidemic of mixed marriages. The Jews of England comprise the second most important Jewish community in the free world. According to Jewish Year Book of 1955 there are about 450,000 Jews in the United Kingdom, of whom 280,000 are in London and the rest (170,000) in the provinces. They are influenced by the general cultural, political, and social life of the country. The majority are departing from traditional Jewish life. Mixed marriages are eliminating entire Jewish families, even communities. There is no Jewish family in England in which either a close or distant relative is not married to a non-Jew. Approximately 15% of all weddings are with non-Jews, not taking into account the civil marriages and those performed by Liberal and Reform rabbis. Dr. I. W. Slo, writing in the "Manchester Guardian," also confirms the ever rising increase of intermarriages in Britain between Christians and Jews.

In France mixed marriage is common not only among the Jews who have lived there for centuries and who have long been French in speech and culture, but also among the children of immigrants from Poland and other parts of Eastern Europe.

In the Scandinavian countries assimilation is widespread. There are many factors that contribute to this state of affairs. Dispersal in small numbers is more common there than in other lands. All doors are open to assimilation; close to 50% of all Jewish marriages are contracted with Christians.

A report about the Jewish community of Stockholm indicates that it comprises 12,000 Jewish souls, is well organized, has a fine *kehillah* building, a large meetinghall, a well-stocked library, and a religious school. The community, however, accounts itself as "half-Jewish." The mixed marriage mania has taken deep root. What will happen, asks the writer of the report, after the death of half-Jews?

The situation is worse in Switzerland. About 20,000 Jews live there. They have no economic worries. Their peaceful mode of life, however, is accompanied by spiritual decline. In the last decade, out of 3,700 weddings among Swiss Jews, 2,500 were contracted out of the faith—a proportion of 70%.

It is no better in the countries with small numbers. There the proportion reaches 40%. In the canton of Basel mixed marriages comprise 40% of all Jewish weddings, and in Brussels the number is higher than that between Jew and Jewess.

No Jewish foot ought to tread again upon the accursed soil of Germany. After the events of 1933–1945 no Jewish community should have been rebuilt there. The actual and unwelcome fact, however, is that more than 22,000 Jews are scattered over Germany. The communities are organized into district associations, and united in a Central Union for the whole country. One-third of those settled are German Jews who lived there before World War II. Many have Christian wives. They have no heirs and no contact with Jewry. Some are *yoredim*—disillusioned returners from Israel. As though for spite many of these have married German fräuleins. Unless something unexpected happens to the death-rate—most of the practicing Jews are aging people—the children will grow up as pure "Aryans" and no Jews will remain in Germany.

Reports from Poland, where a pitiful remnant of 50,000 have remained out of three and a half million, indicate that mixed marriages are increasing. If this process continues, this new *yishuv* will also disappear.

The situation in Soviet Russia is most tragic of all. The threat of spiritual collapse imperils all Russian Jewry. Jewish religion, Jewish culture, Jewish life have been suppressed with brute terror. The process of annihilation of the Jewish spirit follows a deliberate dictatorial blueprint. Those reaching Israel report that a Jewish youth has grown up there totally alienated from all things Jewish. If the Iron Curtain is not lifted and Russian Jewry is not permitted to resume contact with Western Jewry and revive its religion and culture like other ethnic groups there, the continuing process will break the remaining thin thread that still ties Russian

Jewry to the main body of Israel. Furthermore, the situation is no better in the satellite countries, Romania, Czechoslovakia, and Hungary.

In Latin America Jewish communities are fighting with all their might against decline. Integration, the adoption of Latin American manners and customs, and the great number of mixed marriages have led to a situation where in many settlements no Jewish family survives.

In Argentina, where the community is noted for its creativity, the Jews of the provincial areas complain that mixed marriages are as high as 60%. The Jewish community of Brazil, second in Latin America with 120,000, is undergoing a process of assimilation. According to the latest figures of the census bureau, 70,000 have declared themselves of the Mosaic faith. The other 50,000 conceal their Jewish origin. Of the 70,000, about 52,000 live in the two largest cities, Rio De Janeiro and Saõ Paulo. In the provinces the situation is tragic. Mixed marriages no longer constitute a problem there —they are a process.

South Africa too has a high proportion of mixed marriages, though we have no exact figures. At a farewell banquet tendered him by the South African Jewish community, Cecil Tzemach Hyman, the Israeli ambassador, said that the high proportion of mixed marriages was certainly no sign of Jewish national strength.

In Honolulu there is a Jewish settlement of about 300 families. More than half are related to non-Jews through intermarriage. The chief function of the Reform rabbi there is to solemnize these unions and thereby accelerate the liquidation of his own community.

In Lebanon we recently read of the complaints of the chief rabbi, who deplored the large number of unions between Jewish daughters and Moslems.

In Canada, a well organized Jewish community, there are no exact figures. According to the estimates of Louis Rosenbern, statistician, the figure is between ten and twelve percent. Our own estimate based on observation and experience is that the figure is closer to 15%. When one considers that the Jews of Canada are less assimilated and more Jewish than those of the U.S.A., and that work of the Canadian Jewish Congress in the field of culture and education is well developed, then even a figure of 12% is much too high and perilous.

In the U.S.A. there is no Jewish institution interested in determining the percentage of mixed marriages. There are guesses that between 20 and 30% of Jewish marriages in the U.S.A. are out of the faith. When Dr. Louis Finkelstein of the Jewish Theological Seminary uttered a public warning against the rising tide of mixed marriages, he was denounced by the Pollyannas as an alarmist and pessimist.

The actual percentage figures listed here are really not the issue. Let us assume that mixed marriages in Switzerland do not reach 70% but merely 50%, that in England and the U.S.A. the figures throughout are five percent lower. The situation is still packed with enough danger to awaken us all to the threat to Jewish survival.

We live in a time of trying moral and spiritual crises. Yet many of us do not fully grasp the seriousness of the situation. We appease and lull the Jewish public into complacency and shallow optimism. Such indifference to reality will in the end lead to tragic results—unless we awake and summon the Jewish public conscience to its responsibility.

Our complacency and apathy is a dangerous symptom of the times. We should be shaken and filled with unrest. All our resources—social, religious, and communal—must be mobilized to combat the epidemic.

Looking at the fundamental changes in the Jewish way of life, the assimilation that is increasing daily, the will to be submerged and to adopt the practices of the non-Jewish environment, the linguistic assimilation, the sloughing off of Jewish religious values, and the breakdown of the barriers between the faiths, this growing torrent which is demolishing the fences and the hedges which have preserved Judaism until now—one becomes very sad for the future of Jewish life on this continent and throughout the lands of dispersion.

CHAPTER XIII

THE SYNAGOGUE, THE RABBIS, AND PRACTICAL JEWISHNESS

As soon as the Children of Israel received the Torah on Mount Sinai, God bade Moses speak to them, "Let them make a holy place for Me; that I may dwell among them" (Exodus 25:8).

To strengthen the newly granted Torah among the Israelites, to fuse the various tribes into a nation, Divine Providence bade Moses, even before his people set out on their wanderings, to set up a tent wherein the sanctity of the Torah, the faith and unity of Israel, would be centered. Thither the eyes of the new-born Jewish entity would be always turned to remember the bond they formed with God at Mount Sinai.

The Children of Israel erected a tabernacle—a mobile holy structure which they bore with them in the desert. They set it up wherever they halted. It contained the Ark of the Covenant, the two stone tablets upon which were inscribed the Ten Commandments.

The tabernacle served the Children of Israel as a religious center. After settling in the Promised Land, they set up similar sanctuaries in other centers. Here the Holy Presence was to be found and they served as meeting places for national and religious life.

In the Bible the religious center is known as a *mikdash,* a holy place. "They are to make for me a holy place." Rashi comments on this passage in Exodus 25:8, that the words "for me" do not mean that the holy place is to be for God, but for *My name*—a sanctuary where the Jews are to remember that God created heaven and earth, where the Jew is to come to consecrate his thoughts, to feel closer to God, to unite his soul with the divine spirit, and pour out his heart to the Creator. It is also called *mishkan,* from the Hebrew root *shakhan,* to rest. God's resting-place is holy ground for His people. According to the Midrash, the meaning is, "You are my children; I am your Father." It is an honor for children to be near their father, and it is glory for a father to be near his children. Erect a house for thy father so he can be near his children. This is why the Torah states, "Make for me a holy place."

When David ascended the throne, his first step was to construct a Temple. "Behold," he said to Nathan the prophet, "I dwell in a house of pine trees and the ark is hidden behind a curtain" (II Samuel 7). Solomon fulfilled his father's ambition. He built the first Temple and consecrated it to the Lord.

"May Thine eyes be open toward this house by day and by night, to this place where Thou saidest my name to be, to hear the prayer which Thy servant will pray" (I Kings 8:29).

The Temple built by Solomon on Mount Moriah was one of the largest and most magnificent structures in the ancient world. It became the most sacred place, center of the Jewish faith and heart of the Jewish people. The nations of the world acknowledged the sanctity of the Temple, recognized that it was the divine resting-place, and that Jerusalem was the sacred chosen city of the God of Israel.

The Temple served the Jews not only as a place for worship but, like the tabernacle, proved a house of assembly where the religious and national life of the people was concentrated. In time of war and danger the Temple inspired everyone with faith and courage. When the First Temple was destroyed by Nebuchadnezzar and the Second by Titus, the Jews mourned not so much the destruction of the Jewish state as the loss of the Temple. Mourning for the Temple is expressed in all Jewish religion and ceremonial. A special day—the Ninth of Ab—was established not in memory of the lost Jewish Commonwealth but in mourning for the Temple.

After the destruction, the Jews built meeting houses in

every corner of the earth where they found themselves. In each they placed an Ark; in the Ark they set the Scrolls of the Law; and thus they transferred the sacred content of the Temple to the synagogues.

What the tabernacle was in the wilderness and the Temple in Jerusalem, the synagogue became for Jews in all lands of the exile—a holy place wherein Jews become one with their God and with their ancestors, where they come in joy and in sorrow to unburden their hearts.

As often in the course of history, men would turn into beasts who relentlessly pursued their victims. Their savagery was directed mainly against the Jews, who knew they could place no hope on any external powers, for physically they were not capable of halting the murderous hands shedding innocent Jewish blood. They would then assemble in their synagogues, to devote their bodies and souls to the service of the Almighty; they wept, they prayed. We were able to bear inhuman sufferings by virtue of the truth and justice in our faith and our Torah, with confidence that God would not forsake his people, and that salvation would deliver us from the fiery trap.

The deeper the world sank into evil and corruption, the more loftily rang the voice of Jacob in the synagogue. There was built our own spiritual world of heroism like a wall of armor. The greater the storm of license and brutality without, the closer we leaned upon our religious fortresses.

The synagogue still is the Jewish people's center of spiritual life. It was there that the original and authentic Jewish philosophies were crystallized and cultivated. Within its walls the Jew always found a refuge and sanctuary from the winds of alien cultures. The walls of the *bet hakenesset*—the synagogue—prevented the Jewish nation from being absorbed, and saved it from spiritual annihilation.

Jews always felt it was they who needed the synagogue, not the synagogue which had need of them. It brought them belief, inner meaning, a link with the Absolute, eternal union with the God of Israel and the community of Israel. The prayers of the synagogue bring light to his soul, bring him closer to the mysteries of the universe, bestow happiness and spiritual satisfaction. No matter how often he attends, and prays, and praises God, he never has done enough. "Even if our mouths be as full of song as the sea, our tongues have as many praises as the waves of the sea, our lips as the firmament of heaven, we cannot give to God enough thanks for the millions of good deeds he has done for our forefathers and for us." Going to the shul, and worshiping as part of a collective group, the Jew did not feel he was doing anyone a favor but himself. He felt that he enjoyed the synagogue rather than that the synagogue reaped any benefit from him.

For generations Jews derived not only their holiness from the synagogue but also personal pleasure. How keen was the Jew's happiness when he awoke early in the morning to pray in unison with his fellows. How much joy and satisfaction he derived from the period between Minchah and Maariv (afternoon and evening) services! He felt delight and ecstasy in the Sabbath and festivals. It never occurred to him that by going to the synagogue he was maintaining it, that he was supporting Judaism or that the future of Judaism depended upon him. Through all the generations he went to his synagogue, prayed collectively, followed the customs of Judaism for his own sake, for his own satisfaction.

In recent years major changes have come about in Jewish life. Jews attend "to maintain and help the synagogue." Jews pray in order to ensure a *minyan;* Jews make efforts to preserve the Sabbath and festivals; Jews give money to support Jewishness. Judaism has become dependent on Jews. Jews are constantly contributing for their faith, for their fellow Jews. For themselves, however, they take nothing, for seemingly they need nothing. . . .

A feeling of superiority, that the Jew is superior to his religion, that the individual is higher in the scale of values than the community, is seen in the attitude and actions of the present generation of Jews; it exists even among those who have a closer link with the synagogue and Jewish observance.

The Jew who attends synagogue on the Sabbath and who participates in synagogue activities feels that he is working on behalf of the synagogue. He contributes his time, energy, and money, and in return he expects the synagogue and Jewry to be grateful to him. The same applies to observing kashrut and other laws and customs. Modern Jews consider that they are making personal sacrifices to contribute to the maintenance of Judaism—and not that Judaism maintains and keeps *them* together. When a Jew attends the synagogue on the high holy days nowadays, he feels he has bestowed a gift. He is proud of his achievement. The synagogue should thank him. He is a philanthropist.

This attitude never before existed. Jews—even the martyrs who died through *kiddush hashem*—never felt that they were making a concession, or sacrificing for preservation of their faith. In all generations Jews practised Judaism for its own sake. Jewishness was inseparable from one's life. It was not on the periphery.

Responsibility is borne to a great extent by those who speak or write of, and otherwise deal with, Jewry's religious questions, in particular our spiritual leaders. Of this there is not the slightest doubt.

Most Jewish religious leaders, those who identify themselves with Jewish spiritual matters, deal with these abstractly. Jewishness is to them a thing of pure spirituality; they make no effort to demonstrate the personal, almost physical, satisfaction which Jews have always felt in pursuing Jewishness.

Jewish observance has been a source not only of spiritual inspiration but also of mundane pleasure, for the Jew and his family. The preparations for the Sabbath, the celebrations of the festivals, have brought happiness into the Jewish home. The domestic preliminaries for the Passover, the building of a *sukkah* by hand, the purchase of an *esrog*—these were not done with the conscious purpose of "preserving Judaism," but for one's own satisfaction and enjoyment. There was physical contentment in religion at its highest.

The Jew of today derives little personal enjoyment from the observances. The totality of Jewishness is now spanned by the four walls of the synagogue under the authoritarian supervision of the rabbi. Even the traditional Passover seder, which for generations served as a focus for the family re-union, is today "solemnized" in the synagogue under the guidance of a rabbi, or in another public place under the "musical direction" of a cantor. Outside of the synagogue premises the Jew practises very little Judaism. The rabbi serves his congregation as official pronouncer of the *hamotzi* blessing before meals. He practises a vicarious Judaism for his congregation.

A "surrogate-psychology," totally foreign to the Jewish spirit, is in process of formation. The observance of Sabbath and festivals, kashrut, Jewish education, Jewish needs—all these are responsibilities of the rabbi.

The rabbi carries out his members' Jewish duties for them —"I pay you and you fulfill my Jewish obligations for me and my children." This is something Judaism has never before known. Judaism assumes no intermediary between God and man. It has never had a priesthood to represent the mystic bond of faith, as do other religions. The function of the rabbi has always been to interpret Jewish law. The Torah being a complex legal system with 613 commandments which cover all aspects of human life, the rabbi must possess a thorough familiarity with this Jewish religious code and broad scholarship in Jewish religious, moral, and philosophical views. He serves the Jewish community as authority and guide for the faith and law of Israel, but he cannot in the slightest supplant or substitute those things incumbent upon each individual Jew.

Nor does Judaism recognize any dualism of human life, as is implied by the concepts of "synagogual" and "extra-synagogual." God is not confined to the synagogue, but is present at home, at business, at the factory, on the street, and among people everywhere. The man who does not see God in these places will not find Him at the synagogue either. Attendance at synagogue should mean a continuation of an overall religious and ethical behavior.

Jewishness consists not in what one says about it but in what is done about it. A national and religious Jew is an *active* Jew. Not his words but his deeds, how he lives as an individual and as a member of his group, will enable a future Jewish generation to live and prosper.

Many people are of the opinion that we are standing on the threshold of a religious renaissance in American Jewish life, that there is a trend back to religion. Huge synagogues and lavish temples are being built; congregational memberships are rising; the third Jewish generation on this continent—grandchildren of the immigrants—have felt an urge to turn back to the sources of the Jewish faith which their parents and grandparents seem to have forgot.

It is true that more Jews are attending the synagogue than some years ago. Jewish youth is drawn to the synagogue more than formerly. It has become the backbone of Jewish communal life. This, however, has nothing to do with any religious reawakening. It derives rather from the recent tendency in North American life impelling people to join a religious establishment, to attend church, and in general to identify oneself with one's ancestral religion. This has had the effect of inducing Jews to follow suit, and the so-called rebirth of Judaism is no more than a dilution of the religious idea for the purpose of assisting the individual to accommodate himself into the prevailing framework of society.

Will Herberg in his sociological and religious study, "Protestant, Catholic, Jew," points to a great change in American life. Instead of the theory of cultural pluralism which has prevailed to now, the social evolution of the future will erase the ethnic and cultural distinctions between the various minority groups; the sole difference to remain will be the denominational distinction between Catholic, Protestant, and

Jew. American society will acknowledge a Jewish minority only on the basis of denominational identity. According to Herberg, the American citizen will in time have to choose which of these three he will be attached to. The one who belongs to none of the three will rest in a sort of communal limbo, with no recognized status in society. This hypothesis is probably the important reason for the new identification with the synagogue, the rise in synagogue membership, and the growth of new congregations; but it has very little relationship to heightened religious consciousness.

In his book on American Jewry Oscar Handlin indicates that present-day Jews who attend synagogue do not do so out of piety, but out of a feeling of security which comes from belonging to and being identified with a substantial and recognized group. Some attend to find a source of authority which they need in a time of stress and confusion. Others seek release for their overstrained nerves, or some spiritual repose.

Jewish life and Judaism are constantly being measured by the thermometer of the "outside" atmosphere—the attitude of the non-Jewish world. Our sages long ago declared that the fact that Ahasuerus gave Haman his ring, bidding him do as he wished with the Jews, brought Jews closer to their faith than all the preaching of the forty-eight prophets.

The external repellant forces—disillusionment in the liberalism and progress of the non-Jewish world, and its attitude towards our people—no doubt did strengthen the forces of solidarity and served to bring Jews closer to their people.

For these reasons I maintain that the "back to the synagogue" phenomenon and the greater identification with Judaism do not spring from inner spiritual conflict or consciousness, and least of all indicate any religious resurgence.

A living Judaism has been replaced by a Judaism of "sympathy." It is a symbolic kind of Judaism rather than one of living experience. Large synagogues are built at an expenditure of millions, for the purpose of public effect. Inwardly, however, they are spiritually void. These synagogue and temple structures are mausoleums. Their architecture gives them external beauty; inside they are dead.

Hundreds of synagogues, especially in the provincial centers, are vacant almost the entire year. A *minyan* cannot be convened for prayer on the Sabbath or festivals except for a bar mitzvah, or during the three days of Rosh Hashanah and Yom Kippur. Most of the worshipers on the Sabbath or festivals are older men. The younger come for recital of *kaddish* and *yizkor.* They are bored during the service, for most have lost the little Hebrew acquired by bar mitzvah lessons, and they are relieved when the service is over.

Recently even *kaddish* and *yahrzeit* have lost their significance. When the older Jewish generation dies out no one will remain to take their places on Sabbaths and festivals. Aside from the festive occasions from time to time, the synagogues will be open only during the high holy days. The idea had been that prayers in the English language and a sermon by the rabbi in English would attract the youth to the synagogue. In the end none of these remedies have helped. The rabbi delivers his sermons in the most polished Queen's English about the latest best-seller to an audience of elderly Jews. From his pulpit he can see only gray heads.

American Jewry is divided according to its synagogue membership into Orthodox, Conservative, and Reform. In actual fact, this does not in the slightest reflect any division on the basis of religious conviction. Thousands of members of orthodox synagogues are as far from the orthodox way of life as East is from West. Many members of conservative synagogues have not the least idea of the difference between theirs and an orthodox congregation. And members of Reform temples cannot explain why and wherefore the Jewish religion needs reforming.

Successful synagogues are those with a large membership. Larger synagogues mean greater income from dues and increased social status for their members. There are synagogues and temples—their number is increasing—where a large part of the members do not know the prayers in Hebrew. In these the rabbi carries on. Such a service has no warmth, no ecstasy, no depth or soul. The atmosphere is cold and church-like. The members sit silent and docile in their pews, prayerbooks in hand, repeating after the rabbi an English translation of the Hebrew passages. When he intones a prayer in Hebrew they look blank and pronounce their "Amen."

Addressing a conference of conservative rabbis in Colorado, Dr. Abraham Joshua Heschel, professor of ethics at the Jewish Theological Seminary, said that "The modern synagogues are graves, where prayers receive their decent burial." They have dignity, decorum, and elegance, but one item is lacking—the religious turmoil. There is no rapture, no fire, in the prayers. The worship is cold, stiff, and quite dead. Prayer is something that should represent the innermost essence of a person's emotional being.

Our rabbis are concerned with the problem of church and state. Actually there is much greater separation between our synagogue and God than there is between the synagogue and the state. The synagogue has become the house of speeches, not the house of prayer. We have adopted the principle of praying through an emissary: the rabbi or cantor prays for the congregation.

Certainly identification with a synagogue is a positive development. However, it has nothing to do with religious awakening. Religion and the religious experience is a human individual phenomenon that can occur in a congregation with a minyan which carries on collective prayer.

When our parents prayed—though they did so as a group —each poured out his heart to God in his own expression of emotion, each followed his own nuances of the prayers in an individual, undisciplined way, a spontaneous lament or outcry. It was prayer in unison, but each member strove to reach God separately. Every worshiper expressed his own appeal to the Divine through gesture, word, and intonation. They followed the words of Psalm 145: "The Lord is nigh to all who call upon Him." The Midrash asks, does this mean everyone? and answers that it means all those who truly call to Him. Truly means with all one's heart, with one's own experience and with one's own torment. Today there is totally lacking the individual religious experience, the individual's "calling upon the Lord in his agony" (Psalm 118). The modern synagogues have order and decorum. The rabbi and the English prayerbook have liberated the individual from personal religious rites. The worshipers need only be good congregants—and read from the prayerbook at the rabbi's bidding.

Even the recital of *kaddish* in unison led by the rabbi or sexton, though it has external beauty and cadence, lacks emotional feeling.

"When I say *kaddish* by myself," a young man once told me, "I see before me my dead father and the God of our people. If the rabbi or *shamash* join, I lose the picture of my father and the God of Israel. I can see and hear only the rabbi or *shamash*, and I am distracted by the thought of saying a syllable too quickly or slowly and breaking the rhythm. I feel like a soldier under the rabbi's command. I have no longer any awe or fear of God but only of the synagogue functionary."

For generations the synagogue was a house of prayer, a place where Jews prayed and united their souls with the Creator. The rabbi spoke of Torah and Jewish religion. In the synagogue the Jew sought exaltation and ease. It has today become void of Jewishness, there is no holiness, no spiritual elevation. It seeks attractions to draw a crowd. In place of Torah the rabbi talks of world problems, reviews best-sellers, discusses the latest movie or television programs. A large number explain their attendance apologetically by saying they do it for the sake of their children, i. e., they themselves feel no need to go. The synagogue has become a place only for bar mitzvah, kaddish, and yizkor.

Because of this secularization the danger exists that this formal kind of Jewishness may change the lavish synagogue buildings into entertainment palaces, to provide relaxation and recreation. We were once present at a synagogue where singers of both sexes presented a concert which was applauded as though it were in a theatre.

Respect is gone for the Divine Presence, the deep feeling which the synagogue always represented in Jewish life as the holy place that replaced the Temple. The rabbis bear part of the blame because of their constant compromises of Jewish law, on the surface intended for the good of the Jewish religion. Their modernizing and "adjusting" the faith to the times, necessitating removal of a large number of "antiquated" laws and practices, has led to a "select" Judaism which has lost the profundity, the sense of dedication, and the consciousness of the divine of other days.

This "pick-and-choose" Judaism, the "adjustment" to the time and to the convenience of modern people, has shattered many fundamentals, has removed the spiritual and sacred element from Judaism, and in time is likely to lead to a nominally religious Jewish frame enclosing a non-Jewish content.

There was a time in Jewish history when Jews tried to create an "easy" Judaism, which would be acceptable even to non-Jews. They preached that pure religion, a mere formula of good will, is enough to constitute a Jew. The results are well-known. Instead of Jewish posterity, this idea bore a new religion, which for two thousand years has persecuted Judaism and cost us millions of victims.

The same error is being made today by many Jewish religious leaders, who think that by making Judaism easier, by freeing Jews of most of the commandments of the Torah and tradition, Jews will remain Jews and render Jewish existence secure. Judaism as pure religion without the *mitzvot* of the Torah, without the traditional Jewish laws and customs, without specific ceremonial and ritual, is an abstract, empty, disembodied kind of Jewishness which lacks the power of holding the people together as a united flock.

We live in a wealthy, highly civilized country with a broad, well-developed culture. All the mainstreams of this culture flow counter to our practical Jewishness. To keep our identity we must constantly struggle not only against the non-Jewish

environment, but must build powerful spiritual dams to preserve our Jewish identity and Jewish continuity.

Recently Jewish communities have begun to build "syna-
gogue-centers," a synthesis of a place of worship, a school,
and an institution for social and communal activities. These
have expanded, and now claim the central position as community institutions, which parallel the synagogue in fulfilling
their members' Jewish interests. Our experience has been
that the activity and character of the Jewish center consist
mainly in recreational and sport programs.

We do not wish to belittle recreation and sports. They are
quite important, particularly for youth. But we see that in
the activities of the Jewish centers, Young Men's Hebrew
Associations, synagogues, and temples, Jewish culture and
studies—even in the English language—have been relegated
to obscurity. The Jewish child tries to escape when he hears
that the center will be serving a teaspoonful of Jewish studies
or will provide a lecture on Jewish culture.

Those who see in the synagogue-center a symbol of Jewish
unity—a fusion of synagogue, Talmud Torah, and community institution—are in grave error. On the contrary, this
amalgamation underlines that there are no longer Jews with
an ideal, ready to fight for their own particular way of life
and principles. It is a sign that the special modes and principles which made Jewish life so colorful, dynamic, and
vibrant, have vanished.

This union under one roof demonstrates the atrophy of
Jewish life. A center exists for the purpose of bringing people together in a Jewish milieu, carrying on fund raising
drives, organizing brotherhood and interfaith meetings, conducting sports for youth. This is the sum total of its Jewishness. There is no religion, no ideal, no Jewish fulfilment, no
concentration of principles and truths.

Our spiritual leaders deliver speeches about democracy,
humanity, anti-defamation, goodwill, and brotherhood, but
very rarely about history, morals, philosophy, ethics, faith
and practice.

Immediately after destruction of the Second Temple, when the Jews were dispersed over the world, our sages planned a way of life for Jewish survival. The Torah became Jewish land, the religion the Jewish state. When we wrestled against physical annihilation our spiritual leaders always stood on the lookout to see that we did not profane our soil—the Torah—and abandon our state—the Jewish religion.

There are spiritual leaders who maintain that the basis of Judaism is its universal prophetic ideals, and who look down their noses upon practical Judaism, the mitzvot. To them deeds are less important and unworthy in comparison with the "spirit" of Judaism. They make the same errors as the Haskalah movement, not seeing the vacuum into which everything falls. A large number of children whose fathers were maskilim—disciples of the Haskalah—married non-Jews; some were converted; some of these became irreconcilable Jew haters.

For, however true it may be that Judaism's greatest contribution and basic principle is the idea of monotheism, it is not the idea of one God in itself that makes a Jew Jewish, but execution and fulfilment of Torah. The abstract idea of monotheism would in itself not have been able to command the life and thoughts of the Jewish people, or maintained the Jews as a cohesive entity, if we had not been bound by the Torah of Sinai and the whole system of practical Jewishness.

"Jewishness without Sinai," said Dr. Heschel, "is senseless. Why should I be a religious Jew, why should I remain a Jew, go to pray in the synagogue, if the Torah is nothing more than the national literature of the Jewish people?"

Judaism is an idea which calls for practical *fulfilment*. Its abstraction is the Torah, its realization the mitzvot, rules, judgments, prescriptions, as expressed in the Torah. The commandments, rules, and judgments were the contents, the quintessence of faith and people. The keepers of this idea were the bearers of historic Judaism. Those, however, who have taken upon themselves the mission of carrying on the religion, but who prefer to relinquish the rules, remain outside the camp of Israel, cut off from the living people. Their children have married non-Jews, vanished among the general population.

Even when the Jews dwelt in their own land there was no lack of those who preached separation between idea and fulfilment. Neither the Samaritans who remained in Israel, nor the Karaites, and certainly not the Christians, were supporters of historic Judaism. Though these movements stemmed from Judaism and claimed to be true Judaism, none gave aid to Jewish survival—only those who held that "The Law and Israel are one and indissoluble."

There is no point in talking about Jewish spirit and overlooking Jewish life and reality. The Jewish spirit never came to anyone out of sheer talk; it required action, demanded mitzvot—deeds.

Torah and mitzvot were never a burden to the Jews, a privilege not granted other nations. Jews practised Judaism not consciously to support or preserve the Jewish people, but out of deeply felt love for the Torah and its laws, and the happiness and satisfaction they provided.

The Jewish concept of happiness is different from that of other peoples. The Jew did not seek happiness in external things but within himself. He saw his greatest joy in purity, sanctification, the wholeness of his personality, the purity of family life.

We can picture a Jewish consciousness in America and Canada, but we cannot picture the Jewish consciousness existing without Jewish deeds. We are not at all as poor in thought as in the right kind of deeds. It is not so much that our children know so little of Jewishness but that they practise so little.

Judaism without the Jewish way of life is a hollow abstraction, a cobweb. How many Jews have received any real education from the sermons of those rabbis who talk constantly about Jewish monotheism, the Jewish mission, the Jewish spirit, our prophetic universalism? The Jew who disposes of his Judaism with talk alone, but who practises no concrete and practical Judaism, and whose private life differs little from the non-Jew's, has no Jewish physiognomy. His is a Judaism without the breath of life, devoid of heart and soul.

When our parents and grandparents spoke of Judaism, they did not mean Jewish spirit, they meant mitzvot. They understood that an idea without something to clothe it in has no endurance or meaning. They knew that first comes the deed—the idea will be sure to follow. The important thing was to live and act as a Jew. The consciousness of lofty Jewish spirituality would come later.

Judaism is not a matter of taste or feeling which can be maintained on pure thought, however well-intended. The vital elements in Judaism are the deeds, the rules, the laws, as they have been practised and observed.

"A spiritual awakening is taking place among American Jews," said Rabbi Robert Gordis, professor of the Jewish Theological Seminary, at a conference of conservative synagogues in New York, "but it is up to us. It is up to the leadership to what extent it means to exploit the heightened interest in religion and spiritual values. The revival taking place is still a superficial one. We must see that American Jews start living a Jewish life not only through the synagogue and through their organizations and institutions but in their home and through their children. Practical Judaism must become the most vital part of American Jewish life."